OPPOSING
VIEWPOINTS®
SERIES

Street Teens

Other Books of Related Interest:

Opposing Viewpoints Series
Teen Drug Abuse

At Issue Series
Teen Sex

Current Controversies Series
Teen Pregnancy and Parenting

"Congress shall make no law ... abridging the freedom of speech, or of the press."

First Amendment to the US Constitution

The basic foundation of our democracy is the First Amendment guarantee of freedom of expression. The Opposing Viewpoints Series is dedicated to the concept of this basic freedom and the idea that it is more important to practice it than to enshrine it.

OPPOSING VIEWPOINTS® SERIES

Street Teens

Dedria Bryfonski, Book Editor

GREENHAVEN PRESS
A part of Gale, Cengage Learning

GALE
CENGAGE Learning™

Detroit • New York • San Francisco • New Haven, Conn • Waterville, Maine • London

1/12

707965585

GALE
CENGAGE Learning

Elizabeth Des Chenes, *Managing Editor*

© 2012 Greenhaven Press, a part of Gale, Cengage Learning.

Gale and Greenhaven Press are registered trademarks used herein under license.

For more information, contact:
Greenhaven Press
27500 Drake Rd.
Farmington Hills, MI 48331-3535
Or you can visit our Internet site at gale.cengage.com

For product information and technology assistance, contact us at

Gale Customer Support, 1-800-877-4253
For permission to use material from this text or product, submit all requests online at www.cengage.com/permissions

Further permissions questions can be emailed to permissionrequest@cengage.com

Articles in Greenhaven Press anthologies are often edited for length to meet page requirements. In addition, original titles of these works are changed to clearly present the main thesis and to explicitly indicate the author's opinion. Every effort is made to ensure that Greenhaven Press accurately reflects the original intent of the authors. Every effort has been made to trace the owners of copyrighted material.

Cover Image copyright © David Butow/Corbis.

LIBRARY OF CONGRESS CATALOGING-IN-PUBLICATION DATA

Street teens / Dedria Bryfonski, book editor.
    p. cm. -- (Opposing viewpoints)
    Includes bibliographical references and index.
    ISBN 978-0-7377-5761-3 (hardcover : alk. paper) -- ISBN 978-0-7377-5762-0 (pbk. : alk. paper)
    1. Runaway teenagers. 2. Social work with youth. I. Bryfonski, Dedria.
    HV1421.S774 2011
    362.77'5692--dc23
                                                                        2011021024

Printed in the United States of America
1 2 3 4 5 6 7 15 14 13 12 11

Contents

Why Consider Opposing Viewpoints?   11

Introduction   14

Chapter 1: Why Do Teens Run Away?

Chapter Preface   19

1. Teens Run Away to Gain Control of Their Lives   21
   Ruby J. Martinez

2. Street Teens Are Not in Control of Their   35
   Own Lives
   Noam Schimmel

3. Teens Run Away for Many Reasons   50
   Julie Mehta

4. Gay and Transgender Teens Are at Increased   56
   Risk of Becoming Street Teens
   Nicholas Ray

5. Kids Are Running Away Because of   65
   the Bad Economy
   Ian Urbina

Periodical and Internet Sources Bibliography   73

Chapter 2: What Are the Consequences of Being a Street Teen?

Chapter Preface   75

1. Street Teens Often Turn to Prostitution   77
   to Survive
   R. Barri Flowers

2. Many Street Teens Become Physical   88
   or Sexual Victims
   Maureen Blaha

3. Gay and Transgender Street Teens Are at Greater
   Risk of Becoming Sexual Victims   92
   *James M. Van Leeuwen, Susan Boyle, Stacy
   Salomonsen-Sautel, D. Nico Baker, et al.*

4. Many Street Teens Indulge in Risky   97
   Sexual Behavior
   *M. Rosa Solorio, Doreen Rosenthal, Norweeta G.
   Milburn, Robert E. Weiss, Philip J. Batterham,
   Marla Gandara, and Mary Jane Rotheram-Borus*

Periodical and Internet Sources Bibliography   105

Chapter 3: How Can Street Teens Be Helped?

Chapter Preface   107

1. The UK Should Emulate the US Model   109
   for Sheltering Street Teens
   Kira Cochrane

2. US Shelters Are Inadequate for the Needs   116
   of Street Teens
   Martha Irvine

3. Street Teens Are Better Off in Foster   123
   or Group Homes
   Meghan Stromberg

4. Older Teens Cycle Out of Foster Care   137
   and Return to the Streets
   Carol Smith

5. Street Families Can Make Street Teens Safer   150
   Joanne O'Sullivan Oliveira and Pamela J. Burke

6. Street Families Can Make Street Teens   157
   More Violent
   Rene Denfeld

Periodical and Internet Sources Bibliography   165

Chapter 4: Are Street Teens a Global Problem?

Chapter Preface   167

1. Street Youth Are Vulnerable and Need   169
   to Be Saved
   Kevin Clarke

2. Many Street Teens Are Resilient and Adapt   173
   Well to Street Life
   Macalane J. Malindi and Linda C. Theron

3. Street Children Are Often Victims   178
   of Police Brutality
   Evgenia Berezina

4. Street Youth Are a Menace to Society in Nigeria   186
   Toye Olori

5. Community Nurses Can Help UK Street Teens   191
   Alison Moore

Periodical and Internet Sources Bibliography   196

For Further Discussion   197

Organizations to Contact   199

Bibliography of Books   204

Index   206

Why Consider Opposing Viewpoints?

> *"The only way in which a human being can make some approach to knowing the whole of a subject is by hearing what can be said about it by persons of every variety of opinion and studying all modes in which it can be looked at by every character of mind. No wise man ever acquired his wisdom in any mode but this."*
>
> *John Stuart Mill*

In our media-intensive culture it is not difficult to find differing opinions. Thousands of newspapers and magazines and dozens of radio and television talk shows resound with differing points of view. The difficulty lies in deciding which opinion to agree with and which "experts" seem the most credible. The more inundated we become with differing opinions and claims, the more essential it is to hone critical reading and thinking skills to evaluate these ideas. Opposing Viewpoints books address this problem directly by presenting stimulating debates that can be used to enhance and teach these skills. The varied opinions contained in each book examine many different aspects of a single issue. While examining these conveniently edited opposing views, readers can develop critical thinking skills such as the ability to compare and contrast authors' credibility, facts, argumentation styles, use of persuasive techniques, and other stylistic tools. In short, the Opposing Viewpoints Series is an ideal way to attain the higher-level thinking and reading skills so essential in a culture of diverse and contradictory opinions.

In addition to providing a tool for critical thinking, Opposing Viewpoints books challenge readers to question their own strongly held opinions and assumptions. Most people form their opinions on the basis of upbringing, peer pressure, and personal, cultural, or professional bias. By reading carefully balanced opposing views, readers must directly confront new ideas as well as the opinions of those with whom they disagree. This is not to simplistically argue that everyone who reads opposing views will—or should—change his or her opinion. Instead, the series enhances readers' understanding of their own views by encouraging confrontation with opposing ideas. Careful examination of others' views can lead to the readers' understanding of the logical inconsistencies in their own opinions, perspective on why they hold an opinion, and the consideration of the possibility that their opinion requires further evaluation.

Evaluating Other Opinions

To ensure that this type of examination occurs, Opposing Viewpoints books present all types of opinions. Prominent spokespeople on different sides of each issue as well as well-known professionals from many disciplines challenge the reader. An additional goal of the series is to provide a forum for other, less known, or even unpopular viewpoints. The opinion of an ordinary person who has had to make the decision to cut off life support from a terminally ill relative, for example, may be just as valuable and provide just as much insight as a medical ethicist's professional opinion. The editors have two additional purposes in including these less known views. One, the editors encourage readers to respect others' opinions—even when not enhanced by professional credibility. It is only by reading or listening to and objectively evaluating others' ideas that one can determine whether they are worthy of consideration. Two, the inclusion of such viewpoints encourages the important critical thinking skill of objectively evaluating an author's credentials and bias. This evaluation will illuminate an author's reasons for taking a particular stance on an issue and will aid in readers' evaluation of the author's ideas.

It is our hope that these books will give readers a deeper understanding of the issues debated and an appreciation of the complexity of even seemingly simple issues when good and honest people disagree. This awareness is particularly important in a democratic society such as ours in which people enter into public debate to determine the common good. Those with whom one disagrees should not be regarded as enemies but rather as people whose views deserve careful examination and may shed light on one's own.

Thomas Jefferson once said that "difference of opinion leads to inquiry, and inquiry to truth." Jefferson, a broadly educated man, argued that "if a nation expects to be ignorant and free . . . it expects what never was and never will be." As individuals and as a nation, it is imperative that we consider the opinions of others and examine them with skill and discernment. The Opposing Viewpoints Series is intended to help readers achieve this goal.

David L. Bender and Bruno Leone,
Founders

Introduction

> *"The realities of life on the street are not the least bit romantic. But to a teenager who feels trapped and rejected, running away may feel like the only option."*
>
> —*Lawrence Kutner*

There are between 100 and 150 million street children worldwide. Behind these large numbers are a variety of categories of children—runaways, throwaways, children who are part of the child welfare or foster care systems, young single mothers, sex-trade workers, drug dealers and users, and panhandlers. According to Street Connect, a website for homeless and street-involved youth, "street youths are generally understood to be young individuals who do not have a permanent place to call home, and who instead spend [a] significant amount of time/energy on the street (e.g., in alleyways, parks, storefronts, dumpsters, etc.); in squats (located usually in abandoned buildings); at youth shelters and centers; and/or with friends (typically referred to as 'couch surfers')."

While a growing problem, street youth are not a new problem. Homeless and runaway children have existed in the United States since its early pre-nationhood settlement in the 1600s. Worldwide, there are records of abandoned children at the beginning of the Roman Empire more than two thousand years ago. Street youth have been romanticized in books such as Rudyard Kipling's *Kim*, set in late nineteenth-century India, and Charles Dickens's *Oliver Twist*, set in early nineteenth-century London. Society's response to homeless children has changed over the years, as have the reasons children become homeless.

Street Connect finds four times in the history of the United States where homeless children have received significant attention—following the industrial revolution in the mid- to late nineteenth century, which created economic dynamics resulting in family upheaval; during the Great Depression, which began in 1929; during the counterculture movement of the 1960s; and in the period from the mid-1970s to the present day.

Writing about the late nineteenth century and into the early twentieth century, Sara A. Brown, in "Rural Child Dependency, Neglect, and Delinquency," cites the death of parents, abusive home life, divorce, developmental disabilities, delinquency, and poverty as the major reasons children ran away from home. During this time, runaway children were often referred to as waifs and were categorized with hobos, beggars, and bums, according to Peggy A. Shifflett in "Homeless Children and Runaways in the United States." The early twentieth century was a time when it was common to differentiate between the deserving and undeserving poor. According to Shifflett:

> Children who had lost their homes due to societal conditions fell into the category of deserving poor; runaway children who chose to leave their homes, for whatever reason, fell into the category of undeserving poor. Only deserving homeless children were viewed as unfortunate and in need of human services and caring intervention. Runaway children were viewed as vagrants and criminals deserving punitive forms of intervention from people trying to rid themselves and their environment of spoiled goods. This attitude resulted in homeless children and runaways being abused and used as cheap labor by agriculturalists and industrialists.

The Great Depression swelled the ranks of homeless children to two hundred fifty thousand, as many families were unable to provide for their children, and the children took to the streets to find ways of supporting themselves. The Great Depression ushered in an era of social reform called the New

Deal of the Franklin D. Roosevelt administration. Attitudes toward homeless children began to soften, and programs such as the Federal Emergency Relief Administration were established to provide shelters and camps for homeless youth.

Another surge in young people leaving home and living on the street occurred during the counterculture era of the 1960s. The major difference between this group of young people and their predecessors was economic—most of these street youth were well educated and from middle- to upper-class backgrounds. The reasons for leaving home or school for the streets were also different from earlier eras. Instead of escaping abuse or poverty, these young people were attracted to the lifestyle of counterculture communities in urban centers, such as the Haight-Ashbury section of San Francisco and Greenwich Village in New York.

From the early twentieth century through the 1960s, the needs of homeless youth were handled locally through the child welfare agencies or juvenile justice courts. During the mid-1970s, the oversight of homeless youth was shifted to the federal system. According to Anne B. Moses in "The Runaway Youth Act: Paradoxes of Reform," "Runaway youth were nudged on the national agenda in the 1970s by a series of related events, including a considerable rise in their numbers in the 1960s, changing perceptions of the causes of (and cures for) their behavior, and several grisly news stories about their involvement in violent protests or in being beaten, raped, or murdered." In 1974, the US Congress passed the Runaway Youth Act to assist runaways outside the juvenile justice and child welfare systems. The act provides shelter, counseling, educational and vocational training, and health care to runaway, homeless, and street youth.

In 1989, the American Medical Association (AMA) called for research on the health-care needs of homeless and runaway children, stating that homeless and runaway youth should be studied together, since their health needs are the same. This is significant because it ended the AMA's practice of categorizing homeless children as deserving poor and runaway children as undeserving poor.

Social attitudes about street children at the present time reflect a philosophy of positive youth development as promoted by the Family and Youth Services Bureau (FYSB), a part of the US Department of Health and Human Services. According to the FYSB, "the youth development approach is predicated on the understanding that all young people need support, guidance, and opportunities during adolescence, a time of rapid growth and change. With this support, they can develop self-assurance and create a happy, healthy, and successful life."

While the number of street children has increased alarmingly, the United States now has a variety of services and programs to support and assist them. In the viewpoints that follow, sociologists, psychologists, commentators, and journalists offer varying opinions on the issues surrounding street teens in chapters that ask Why Do Teens Run Away? What Are the Consequences of Being a Street Teen? How Can Street Teens Be Helped? and Are Street Teens a Global Problem? The varying viewpoints in *Opposing Viewpoints: Street Teens* give the reader an idea of the complexity and difficulty of the issues surrounding street teens in the new millennium.

CHAPTER 1

Why Do Teens Run Away?

Chapter Preface

The National Runaway Switchboard (NRS) provides an electronic bulletin board teens can access to get advice about the problems that lead them to contemplate running away from home. In a recent posting, a young girl writes she has had to deal with the death of her boyfriend and the divorce of her parents in the past year, while also struggling with ADHD and depression. Another writer says she has been sexually and physically abused at home since she was four years old. When her mother failed to protect her, she turned to a life of alcohol, gangs, and drugs. A 15-year-old girl reports she fell in love with a 19-year-old man on Facebook, and wants to run away to be with him. These posts describe some of the many reasons youth become street teens.

Statistics kept by the NRS indicate a dramatic increase in the number of teens running away or being thrown out of their homes with a rise in the proportion of the latter. And kids are running away at an earlier age. The NRS estimates that each year between 1.6 and 2.8 million US youth will face a period of homelessness.

Typically, family problems such as divorce, remarriage, and problems with siblings are the most common reasons teens run away. Teens who identify as gay, lesbian, bisexual, or transgender often encounter negative reactions from their parents that cause them either to be thrown out or leave their homes. Other reasons teens leave home for the street include neglect and physical or sexual abuse. Economic issues have emerged as a growing problem since 2008, with more and more youth citing the depressed economy as a reason for leaving home.

Covenant House, a privately funded child care agency providing services to homeless and runaway youth, reports the following statistics from the children taking refuge in its shelters:

Nearly 50% reported intense conflict or physical harm by a family member

41% witnessed acts of violence in their homes

19% reported being beaten

19% reported sexual abuse

15% had someone close to them murdered

Although teens encounter danger on the street, many are fleeing home situations that are perilous. Others have no choice, as they are abandoned or rejected by their family. The reasons youth become street teens are debated in the following chapter.

| *"The choice to run is an attempt to exert control over what the teen perceives to be an intolerable situation."*

Teens Run Away to Gain Control of Their Lives

Ruby J. Martinez

A study of runaways in a midwestern city determined that most teens ran away in order to gain control over their lives and escape negative situations, reports Ruby J. Martinez in the following viewpoint. Once they are on the street, teens find they are trading one set of dangers for a new one. Most runaway teens, however, want to regain a connection with their families, Martinez maintains. More services need to be provided to runaway teens that help whole families address the problems at home, she concludes. Martinez is associate professor emeritus in the College of Nursing at the University of Colorado at Denver.

As you read, consider the following questions:

1. What statistics does the author cite to back her contention that homeless teens are at greater risk for substance abuse?

Ruby J. Martinez, "Understanding Runaway Teens," *Journal of Child and Adolescent Psychiatric Nursing*, vol. 19, no. 2, May 2006, pp. 77–88. Copyright © 2006 by John Wiley and Sons. All rights reserved. Reproduced by permission.

2. What are some of the reasons the teens in the study gave for running away, according to the author?

3. Away from home, street teens develop new relationships that help them cope with life on the street. What are some of the benefits and dangers of these relationships, as cited by Martinez?

Despite the many risks and often grievous consequences of habitual run behavior, it remains an acceptable option for too many of our youth. During the year 2002, an estimated 1.6 million U.S. youth aged 12 to 17 had run away from home and slept on the streets. Teens that run away from home rarely have an effective support system and lack needed assistance, resources, and coping strategies for problem solving and conflict resolution.

Running into Risky Situations

The provocations for running away are diverse and distressing, ranging from running to escape physical, emotional, and sexual abuse to having been thrown out of their homes (termed throwaways) by parents unable to cope with their child's substance abuse or sexual orientation. Runaways leave home in search of safety, independence, or a less restrictive environment, a reality that few successfully achieve. Most of these youth are revictimized on the streets. They attempt to survive while engaging in high-risk behaviors such as unprotected sex, drug use, and survival sex. Such behaviors placed these youth at greater risk for victimization by both known (friend/acquaintance) and unknown (stranger) assailants. The often brutal reality of street life is marked by hunger, violence, drugs, and exploitation.

Once homeless, teens are at greater risk for substance use. In one study, 43% of the participants were found to have alcohol and drug abuse disorders across all age and gender categories. Further, the use of alcohol in the past year [2002] was higher among youths who had run away (50%) than those who had not (33%), and use of marijuana and other illicit drugs was higher for runaway youth (27.8% and 23.2%) than those who were not (14.3% and 12.4%).

Mental illness (such as conduct disorder, depression, dysthymia [chronic depression]) was identified in 50% to 73% of youth in runaway samples and in 53% of teens in a juvenile justice sample. Suicide attempts were common (1 in 3) in street youths. [In a 1998 study, B. Molnar, S. Shade, A. Krai, R. Booth, and J. Watters] found that sexual and physical abuse prior to running were independent predictors of suicide attempts. Their study included a pre-run assessment of participants' home life experiences. Seventy percent (70%) of females reported sexual abuse with a mean age of first incident at 9.0 years, half as many reporting physical abuse (35%). Males, on the other hand, reported more physical abuse (35%) compared to sexual abuse (24% with a mean age of first incident at 9.9 years). Seventy-two percent (72%) of females and 51% of males reported suicidal ideation [creating an idea], with 48% of females and 27% of males reporting actual attempts. Their sample showed a clear temporal relationship revealing the abuse occurred prior to the suicidal and runaway behavior.

Runaway teens who were both physically and sexually abused were significantly more vulnerable than those experiencing only physical abuse and suffered with lower self-esteem and personal problems, depression, and suicidal behavior, and engaged in promiscuity and prostitution. Sexually abused female teens were more likely to run at an earlier age and both gender teens engaged in more unprotected sex than those who had not been sexually abused.

Research on runaway teenagers has identified the many dangers these teens faced at home and on the streets. Yet, many teens run repeatedly and it is not clearly known how they provide for themselves day to day while on the run. An exploratory study using a convenience sample of teens incarcerated in a detention center was implemented to better understand run behavior from the teens' perspective and to identify how they maintained personal safety while on the run. Specific research questions included: Why do teens repeatedly run away? How do runaway teens keep themselves safe while on the run? And, how or why do teens stop or end a run? . . .

Changing the Situation

Teens gave clear and specific reasons why they ran from their home or a placement site. All of the teens were attempting to escape an environment or a situation that was unpleasant or dangerous. Many of these young people had grown up with violence and substance abuse in their families, often having to care for themselves or their siblings. Despite the inherent difficulties, the move to the streets was often perceived as being no worse than what they had experienced in their homes. Their memory of what they ran from provided a perspective that helped them to endure hardships while on the run. Changing their situation by running away created many problems for these teens, but their voluntary act of leaving gave them a greater sense of control over their life.

Some teens ran away hoping that running away would somehow change the dynamics at home. By assessing their parents' response to their run, they hoped to find out how their parent really felt about them. Many participants described feeling lonely, unloved, left out, and forgotten. They needed to know if their parent(s) "really cared" for them. JJ explained that he was the middle child and thought that his mother always paid more attention to his siblings. He said, "I just felt I was always left out . . . that is why I felt like running . . . I just felt that I needed to get away . . . that my mom didn't really care about me I wanted to see if she really cared about me if I ran." Josh said he left home when his mother remarried and he did not "get along" with his stepdad. Several teens mentioned wanting to "go party" or "live life on the edge." Lady Adonis ran away with her sister because their mother would not allow them to "party" with friends. When they returned home after being away for a month, their mother not only allowed them to use alcohol and marijuana in the home (as long as they did not use it in front of her), but in some instances, facilitated purchasing them. Lady Adonis reported that her mother "was doing her own thing (with drugs) in the kitchen with her friends and we were sitting in the living room with our friends."

Other teens ran to escape dangerous living situations. Faith said, "The very first time I ran was because my dad was hitting me. There was like drug use and alcohol in my house like almost everyday and I really didn't want to stay there." Starlet said that her mother's life "revolved around drugs" and that her life "revolved around escaping from all that she (her mother) was doing." Vanessa and Haley ran from their homes because of sibling fighting that was getting more intense and violent. Abuse was also reported in the foster home setting. Ceci said that her foster family used racial slurs and "put her down." Michael 1 stated that he would rather live on the streets than to live in a placement.

Runs occurred impulsively with little thought about personal safety, and usually after a negative event. Starlet's comments reflected many of the other teens' responses. She runs "because I try to get away from the situation that I am at . . . to feel like I'm more in control of myself . . . at least I am getting away from that problem . . . Running away was like my problem-solving thing." Alyssa described her run behavior as a "natural instinct." She said, "Everybody in my family calls me a runner. I'm just a runner. As soon as something goes wrong, I run. Or as soon as I feel like I'm gonna get hurt, I run." Michael 2 said that when he ran, he went with only the thought of "getting out," and would worry about food and a

"Something comfortable with good arch support and a cushioned heel. He wants to run away from home."

Mike Baldwin/© Mike Baldwin/Cartoon Stock.

place to stay later, once he was free. Of all the numerous run events described by the teens in this sample, only one person reported preparing for a run by getting a few of her things together before leaving, confirming the spontaneous nature of run behavior. . . .

Creating New Affiliations

Runaway teens engaged in behaviors that created new affiliations with people and substances. These new relationships offered the teen emotional comfort and material assistance for surviving life on the streets. Nicole related a story of a chance meeting in a restaurant with strangers who had a daughter with whom she became close friends. Over time, Nicole was invited to move in with her new friend, and explained, "I've known her (for 10 months) and I seem really close to her and I claim her as my cousin . . . I know her whole family now." Another teen, Jade, said that the people she considers her family are not her blood relatives. She said, "My mom wasn't there, my dad wasn't there, they (her new family) were there . . . they've accepted me into their families, and now I have nieces and nephews."

Sarah formed a close relationship with a friend when her mother was too focused on work and the chemotherapy treatments that she was taking at the time. Sarah said she was raped one night at a teen party but she did not think she could tell her mother about it. Sarah eventually left home to live with this friend who she regarded as her "sister." "When I just tried to talk to her (the mother) about little stuff she would cut me off and start talking about something totally different, like she was scared to hear what I was telling her. And so it was like when I used to go and talk to this girl—I call her my sister . . . every time I talked to her on the phone or something and I would tell her and she would listen to me and all that. So I was like, OK, well, I found somebody that will listen to me. I'm going to stay with her." But too often the initial positive aspects of these new affiliations are replaced with new risks. Sarah was raped a second time when left in a vulnerable situation in her friend's home. Vanessa believed she could turn to her friend's mother, who had also run away frequently as a teen. Vanessa felt she was always welcome to stay in their home when she was on the run but admitted that her friend's mom was a heavy alcohol and drug user.

Gang affiliation was prevalent with this sample of teens. Ten teens in the sample openly admitted membership in a gang, three admitted association with a gang, one teen was "invited to join," and two stated they wanted out of their gang. Only one teen in this sample denied affiliation with a gang. Some have been involved with gangs most of their lives and often regarded their fellow gang members as family. These relationships were experienced by the teens as both protective and dangerous. Ceci described her mentor in the gang in the following way: "Well, actually I was kind of born into the gang. I have family members who are from my gang. My OG (old gang) is like the older sister that I had always wanted . . . she wasn't going to let anybody take me and mistreat me." This teen stated that her gang mentor did not approve of her running away—that she had advised her to stay in school and graduate, but that Ceci did not agree with her mentor and ran anyway. Nicole stated, "When I was around my gang, I felt I had people to trust at the time, and I felt that I could, you know, could trust them more than my father for some reason, like somebody loved me more than my father." Josh said he got into trouble when he started stealing cars and selling drugs with his older gang friends. He was only 14 years old at the time.

Although most teens were able to establish relationships that offered them some level of assistance, support was sporadic. Over time, teens went from home to home, staying with friends or lived on the streets until they were caught or they turned themselves in. Some friends were long-term associates, but there were times when the teen would stay with someone they hardly knew. Alyssa said that she stayed with whoever would accept her for the night. Dana said, "It's not fun to be on your own. And it's not fun to have to struggle and look for a place to stay, move from here to there."

An equally concerning affiliation involved the use and sale of drugs. Teens perceived that drugs helped them endure their different life circumstances. The use of drugs served to mitigate unpleasant feelings and experiences. Problems disclosed by the teens included depression, stress, suicidal behavior, anxiety, bipolar disorder, feelings of anger and rage, conduct disorder, ADHD, and fire-setting behavior. The few teens who had visited a mental health provider often refused to discuss their family problems due to their anger and distrust of the system. They turned instead to drugs to reduce their emotional pain. Nine teenagers reported mental illness, including two who reported suicide attempts.

The sale of illegal drugs allowed the runaway to survive financially on the streets. Ceci explained: "The first time when I ran away it was scary. I didn't know what to do. I didn't know where I was gonna go. I didn't have any clothes. I didn't know what I was gonna eat. It was hard and I felt like a loner, sleeping at other people's houses. But as I ran, it got easier and easier. It was to the point where I was selling drugs. I didn't need anybody. I could buy my own food; I could get my own hotel and you know, buy an outfit every day to put on my back. It wasn't hard anymore, even though I was doing wrong, it was easier because I could depend on drugs to help me get money."

The use of drugs to cope with the stresses of street life provided a false and dangerous sense of security. Teens identified the use of drugs as a form of rebellion, a temporary way of forgetting the pain in their lives or as a way to socialize with their peers. Some, like Vanessa and Kitty, used drugs for the first time when they ran away. Kitty said, "I tried a lot of drugs . . . I wanted a perfect life but knew I'm not going to get it . . . that's why I turned to drugs and everything because I didn't have what I wanted. I wanted to be rebellious and everything." All but one teen reported the use of drugs. In this sample, marijuana and alcohol were most commonly used, but the use of cocaine, acid, mushrooms, ecstasy, and nitrous oxide were also reported.

Learning from Experience

The final category relates to what the teens learned about themselves through their experiences and how these lessons contributed to their decision to stop running. The youth reported that they could not run from their problems, that problems persisted even after they had changed their situation. One teen expressed that when she was on the run she "was just getting sick of it . . . Everywhere I went my problems were still there. I really didn't know what to do." Starlet, who had been in detention five times when she participated in this study, said that she would offer other runaway teens this advice: "Whatever they are running from, doesn't get better until they try to resolve it . . . It just always gets worse." She said that she realized over time that "you are hurting other people when you run, but you're mostly hurting yourself."

The studied youth expressed that despite the problems at home, they often missed their mother or other family members and longed to see their home, their pets, or siblings. Jade said that there were a couple times when she stopped by her mother's house. She added, "I broke into the window so I could get my clothes and my belongings—so I wouldn't get so homesick." Tim Garfield said she returned home "at least every other day, to take a shower or dress up." She explained that she knew when her mother was not home and she went home to eat, shower, and visit with her little brother. Alyssa said "I even missed my brother and my hamster when I am gone. You miss your house, your bed, your parents."

Several of the teens in this study were parents. Michael 1 and Krystle spoke about their children. JJ's girlfriend was pregnant and he expressed a desire to take responsibility to care for his new family. Both Ann and Pam said that they were pregnant and planning to keep their babies. Ann said that having her baby would stop her run behavior. She stated,

"I can't have him living out on the street." Pam reported that she turned herself in because of her pregnancy and concern for her baby.

Never knowing who to trust was difficult for teens because making good decisions about who could be trusted was central to survival. Michael 2 said that he made judgments about people he met on the street based upon their looks. Dana said she began to realize over time that her mother was the one person she could count on, "people that claim to be your friends aren't always there for you when you really need them . . . you're out there by yourself."

Violence and dangerous sexual encounters were prevalent in the lives of the teens. Pam said that a stranger shot at her and her friends "for no reason" when she first ran at the age of 14, and that when men knew she was a runaway, they would try to take advantage of her situation. Jennifer related a situation in which when she attempted to leave a gang member's home, she was locked in against her will. Lady Adonis reported being beaten and raped by an acquaintance one evening while they were both drunk. She did report the rape and although the police did not arrest the man, she was confident that her gang would "deal with him." Jerome recalled a time when he was 14 and on the run overnight. "They'd come up to me (people on the street) and say, 'are you working tonight?' . . . and fondle me . . . I was scared." Jennifer and her girl-friend ran away together and the two girls "stripped" for guys they knew, and would "do drugs with them." The two girls had a safety plan that one of the two of them would always "stay a little sober . . . in case something bad happens." Jade described her life like this: "I was living with my boyfriend and I was constantly smoking weed and I was constantly drinking. There was a time where the people that were in the household that were there had done a robbery on a liquor store . . . and they brought home liquor . . . and cigarettes. At that time, we had like six or seven people who were drug dealers that were coming in and out of the house and the group that I was living in was really bad . . .". Despite their many dangerous experiences, runaways tended to minimize the risks omnipresent in their lives. As Tim Garfield explained, "We may put ourselves in situations, but if we get out of it alive, then it's just another experience."

Although there was an awareness that lost time could not be made up, the teens appreciated that their experiences over the past years were valuable lessons in life. Faith said, "I just wanted to go to school, you know, go to my proms and all of that, graduate and do all those other things. But being on the run I really couldn't do all that stuff, so it kind of ruined it for me." Nicole found the transition back to being a dependent teen a difficult one. She said "It's taken me this long to know what I was doing wrong in the past . . . I am still a kid and I have to listen to other people." Jade said that runaway teens have experiences that they could not have as adults. She said "when you step over that boundary of turning 18 years old, you can't be a runaway anymore."

Changing Family Dynamics

This study found that running, at least initially, is an impulsive behavior set in motion with little regard for personal safety. The act of running is triggered by the desire to achieve immediate relief from an overwhelming physical or emotional burden. The choice to run is an attempt to exert control over what the teen perceives to be an intolerable situation. Teens feel frightened during the first run, but learn quickly that survival depends upon forming relationships with others who will assist them. With practice and the development of street sense, the run experience becomes less frightening, more habitual, and their connection to and comfort with countercultures grows. Runs ended when teens voluntarily went home because they were tired of hiding, missed their family, or when it became too difficult or dangerous to stay on the streets. Others turned themselves in to the police or purpose-fully got caught so that they could return to a detention cen-ter, which was viewed as a safe place of refuge. . . .

The runaway teens in this study raised critical questions when they asked why the "system" (which appeared powerful to the teen) was unable to help their family when it was in crisis, expressing their desire/hope that an intervention could have helped maintain the family structure. Even those who were severely abused wanted to retain some ties with their families. Several teens posed the question, "Did you really help me by taking me away from my family?" From their view-point, they were in a detention center and had endured hard-ship and abuse on the streets; a situation that they felt was ar-guably no better than what they were removed or ran from. The challenge for providers is to create interventions that en-gage the family in behavioral changes that improve interper-sonal relationships and safety for everyone in the home while allowing the family to remain intact. Family-oriented inter-ventions can improve the behavior and psychosocial function of runaways. When families participated in meetings to teach them skills in establishing boundaries and expectations, im-proving parenting and communication, problem-solving skills and assistance in accessing social support systems, the partici-pating youth had lower rates of subsequent alcohol- and drug-related offenses, total delinquency, and crimes against persons. Screening for neglect or abuse within the family should be a part of all obstetric, pediatric, or adult healthcare encounters, especially in higher risk environments where there are known physical or intellectual disabilities, a family history of mental or addictive disorders, multigenerational poverty, divorce or separation, or a prior history of abuse or neglect. Early identi-fication and intervention with at-risk families is essential.

Runaway teens helped identify potential barriers to the utilization of available services and potential motivators to run again. They cited restrictive rules at shelters, concerns regarding disclosing personal information and it remaining confidential (e.g., reports to child protective services), inadequate segregation into age appropriate groups (leading to revictimization), matching services to special needs (e.g., racial/ethnic differences, gay, lesbian), frustrations with high staff turnover (trust/confidence issues) and the need for increased assistance and support to transition off the streets. Much more needs to be done to provide services, including basic healthcare and mental health assessment and treatment, case management, family support services, crisis intervention, educational and vocational training, and life skills training.

> *"The concern for respecting the rights of children to determine where and how they wish to live ... disempowers children by assuming that they choose to live on the street."*

Street Teens Are Not in Control of Their Own Lives

Noam Schimmel

Although some civil rights activists insist on the right of street children to make their own choices, the reality is that most of these children do not have the skills necessary to make informed choices, argues Noam Schimmel in the following viewpoint. Few street children have the education and psychological well-being to make good choices—either about the decision to leave home or how to live on the street. Noam Schimmel is a London-based researcher and human rights practitioner who has written for numerous publications, including the New York Review of Books, *the* Jewish Chronicle, *and the* Jerusalem Post. *He has worked in Africa and Asia on international development and humanitarian relief projects, with a focus on securing the rights of street children and indigenous peoples, and addressing poverty through community development.*

Noam Schimmel, "Freedom and Autonomy of Street Children," *The International Journal of Children's Rights*, vol. 14, 2006, pp. 211–233. Copyright © 2006 by The International Journal of Children's Rights. All rights reserved. Reproduced by permission.

As you read, consider the following questions:

1. What are some of the basic rights delineated in the UN Convention of the Rights of the Child that are not protected when a child lives on the street, according to the author?

2. What are the four basic needs that Abraham Maslow identifies in his hierarchy of human needs, as cited by the author?

3. What are some of the steps governments should take to address the issue of street children, in the author's opinion?

In situations of poverty, neglect, abuse, and desperation—children run away from home and seek a better life on the street. It is a normal human reaction to escape pain and suffering and to seek freedom and safety. However unlikely their realization may be in a hostile and unstable urban environment, to children escaping such home environments, the street can be a compelling alternative that they perceive as offering the chance for a better life. But is the decision of a child living in conditions of emotional and social vulnerability and deprivation to leave home, the reflection of an autonomous individual's free will? I will argue that it is more accurate to define it as a constrained choice—one severely limited by the child's incomplete personal and intellectual development, impoverished background, and the unstable and often hostile environment in which he is living. 'Street children' move from their homes to the street from ages as young as four, through the teenage years. Few have successfully completed their schooling, and many suffer from gaps in their social and cognitive development as a result. The psychologist Abraham Maslow contends that people with such a social background often lose confidence in their most basic abilities, leaving them disempowered and unable to make informed life choices.

This assessment applies both to the initial decision that children make to leave home and escape to the street, and to the 'choice' to remain living on the street that they exercise on a daily basis. . . .

Children Run Away to Meet Basic Needs

Most children move to the street in search of realization of basic needs—and not merely as an escape from the tedium of home life or the desire to express their independence by leaving friends and family. Running away from home is an act of resistance and an expression of absolute frustration with life circumstances. It is the strongest possible response to poverty and abuse that children in circumstances of deprivation and vulnerability can exercise. Their home life and street life are both defined by two major forms of deprivation of basic needs that are essential for healthy child development and socialization: a sound family life defined by supportive parents and intimate relationships, and adequate social provisions of food, shelter, clothing, and quality schooling. Typically, neither in the homes where they previously lived, nor on the streets where they have come to establish a new life are these needs met.

I will argue that living on the street on a full-time basis endangers the lives of children and is developmentally incapacitating; street life fosters feelings of disempowerment and social disconnection and results in psychological distress and emotional instability. I will draw upon the humanist psychologist Abraham Maslow's conception of the *Hierarchy of Human Needs* to show how street life actively frustrates and often makes impossible the realization of these basic human needs. I will argue that Amartya Sen and Martha Nussbaum's concept of promoting the development of human capabilities should be applied to street children, and that living on the street prevents children from realizing these capabilities.

I will show that street children experience high levels of stress and of physical and sexual abuse and psychological trauma as a result of living on the street, and that they suffer from psychological pathologies such as depression and suicidal behaviour at substantially higher rates than children who live at home or in alternative permanent accommodation. Finally, I will argue that although residential care is not an ideal environment for children, it is legally and morally obligatory upon governments to place street children in residential care to ensure their safety and that their basic rights and needs are met. Sometimes this may require the local department of social services to exercise force in the best interests of the child and remove him from the street, even against his will. When done with sensitivity to the child, and in accordance with the human rights guarantees delineated in the UN Convention on the Rights of the Child (CRC), such action is prudent and of urgent importance because the longer a child lives on the street, the greater his tendency to exhibit symptoms of psychopathology. The human right to which the CRC gives priority is that of the survival of the child. The provisions of his basic food, shelter, and healthcare needs as guaranteed in Articles 24 and 27 of the CRC are constituents of that right, and they cannot be assured while a child is living on the street.

Assessing a child's capacity for autonomous self-expression, particularly a child that runs away from a distressed family life and moves to the street, is crucial for the development of sound social policy and the successful administration of social services to children that live on the street. It some cities with large populations of street children in the developing world, government agencies and NGOs [nongovernmental organizations] characterize a child's existence on the street as the result of a free choice that he made, a choice that ought to be respected by the government. Such an argument often focuses on the civil rights of the child guaranteed by the CRC, and bases itself on the primacy of protecting a child's liberty, and his right to have his life choices respected, in particular, his rights to freedom of mobility and freedom of association. I argue that this interpretation of the CRC is wrong; that it fails to secure the child's social and economic rights to food and shelter—rights which ensure his physical and psychological well-being which are necessary conditions for him to exercise autonomy and experience freedom; and that it does not recognize that a child's decision to remain on the street is often a result of an adaptive preference based on a harmful social reality defined by the violations of a child's rights. . . .

The concern for respecting the rights of children to determine where and how they wish to live, while often well-intentioned in origin, disempowers children by assuming that they choose to live on the street, instead of challenging the social conditions that cause them to escape to the street and make it a virtually inevitable alternative of last resort for them. It ignores the legal basis for the indivisibility of human rights guaranteed by the CRC, and, by prioritizing the civil rights of children undermines their most fundamental right—the right to life, which can only be assured by providing them with their social and economic rights and placing them in an environment where they will not be subject to physical and sexual abuse. . . .

Defining Freedom and Autonomy

Freedom can only be exercised in situations in which individuals have the capability to reason and act autonomously in an informed manner, without constraining influences such as drugs/inhalants, coercion and intimidation, and their own limited cognitive and emotional development to constrict their understanding of the choices before them, and the short- and long-term consequences of those choices. They must be able to think and judge potential choices critically. [According to Stanley Benn:]

The concept of a person is intimately bound up with agency. A person is one who envisages and initiates actions ... to initiate an action is to have a kind of causal independence that arises out of the subject's having his own understanding of the nature and significance of his behaviour, and from that understanding's being causally necessary to the agent's performance.

Street children are rarely in a position to initiate such actions, and often allow their emotions and impulses to dominate their judgments. In the lives of street children, their almost total lack of access to schooling precludes their adequately developing their practical reasoning skills. . . .

According to the psychologist Abraham Maslow, for a person to actualize his full potential there are four basic needs that must be met: Physiological, safety, love, and esteem needs. These are all prerequisites for what Maslow defines as a person's self-fulfilment of his talents and capacities, his 'self-actualization.' These needs are organized in a pyramidal hierarchical structure; only when the most basic survival needs of food, shelter, and safety are met can an individual progress to achieve the needs that follow, the love and esteem needs. An individual will always seek to fulfill the basic needs first, and will join whatever community that can provide him with the realization of these needs. Thus a child living on the street is likely to join a gang or a group of other street children that assist him to meet his own needs on his first few days living on the street. He will be focused exclusively on his survival needs and having found a way to meet some or most of them, he will not want to risk giving up his present condition of relative security by moving to a shelter.

The physiological needs of a child are not met with regularity on the street because of the lack of reliability of food supply and its often dubious nutritional value. Street children also often lack suitable shelter, clothing during winter to keep warm, and adequate facilities for bathing. They also lack medi-

Jewel Was a Street Teen

I have a personal understanding of the plight of these young people on the margins, because I experienced homelessness firsthand. . . .

When my story is told in the music press, it can take on a romantic glow but living in a van was not romantic. . . .

I do not believe America's homeless youth population is made up of children who leave home because they want to. Most homeless kids are on the streets because they have been forced by circumstances to believe that they are safer alone than in the home they once knew—if that home even exists for them anymore.

Jewel, "Street Life Is No Life for Children,"
USA Today Magazine, *November 2007.*

cal care and thus their physiological needs are not assured living on the street. The safety needs of children are not assured on the street because of the high rate of violent crime that street life entails, and the high prevalence of physical and sexual abuse on the street. The love and esteem needs of street children are rarely met because they do not have the opportunity to develop close relationships with adults who they can trust and count on for unconditional love and support, and because they are stigmatized by living on the street. . . .

Maslow's theory of the hierarchy of human needs and his analysis of the ways in which human beings prioritize these needs and pursue the most fundamental ones, illustrate that street children do not choose the street. Rather, they are generally forced into moving to the street because they perceive it to be (and it often indeed is the case) the only place where they can achieve some of their basic needs and extricate themselves from the oppressive experiences from which they are suffering at home. Maslow's observation that individuals only yearn consciously for what they believe can be obtained supports Korgaard's conviction that street children do not exercise choice by living on the street, because they often lack the capacity to recognize alternatives to the street and adapt their life preferences to a street environment characterized by multiple deprivations.

Street Children Lack Autonomy

For autonomy to be a meaningful concept it needs to be defined with ample attention paid to the environmental and social context in which it is to be exercised. Some academic literature examining the concept of choice in the lives of street children defines autonomy simply as the ability to make a choice between more than one life option. Arnon Bar-On, for example, insists that street children's autonomy should be respected; arguing that they consciously and deliberately choose to live on the street, and that there is a moral and legal case for respecting this choice:

> To respect others as autonomous beings is to treat them as capable of agency, which at a minimum means that we allow them, in some situations, to make the choices that will determine what happens to them and how they conduct their life, and that our responses to them are responses that respect their choices . . .

But Bar-On does not take into account the context of this choice, and he does not define a minimum criterion for freedom. He says that because some parents are unable to fulfill their responsibilities to their children, and because some governments are unable or unwilling to do so, 'Certain children, therefore, have taken to pursuing their own standard of living by appropriating adulthood. They have, in effect, empowered themselves . . . they have done so apparently with little or no damage to society, or to themselves.' Bar-On is right to characterize their move to the street as an attempt at empowerment. But he does not qualify this statement with an analysis of whether or not this attempt at empowerment succeeds. Indeed, it usually fails. Beyond the short-term achievement of removing a child from an abusive and/or poverty stricken family situation, the street is an equally disempowering and harmful context in which to grow up where street children are unable to develop their capabilities to any substantive degree. . . .

Why Interference Is Necessary

Once a child has become socialized into street life, it becomes an extremely difficult space from which to extricate himself. Having experienced a certain type of extreme freedom, having developed friendships and social networks, and having used drugs and glue, children will often be resistant to leave the street. In addition to harming the physical health of children, drugs can severely compromise their mental capacities and ability to make informed choices. Street children will often acknowledge that they feel reviled by the public, 'The public say bad things like for me to get out of here. It makes me feel bad. It makes me feel like garbage. Like I'm not worth anything.' And yet, even living in this context of having their sense of self-worth attacked on a regular basis, street children do not perceive themselves as having an alternative to the street. They desperately want to be respected and loved—but they lack the confidence and resources needed to leave the street and move to a shelter.

There are four major ways in which the choices of a child that lives on the street are severely constrained:

a. adaptive/perverse preferences

b. learned helplessness

c. incapacity to envision a better future

d. lack of information on how to achieve such a future and lack of support to achieve such a future.

To the extent that a child chooses to live on the street, his choice typically reflects an *adaptive preference* or a *preference deformation*. Adaptive preferences are formed 'without one's control or awareness, by a causal mechanism that isn't of one's own choosing.' The negative freedom that street life affords, its familiarity and lack of formal regimentation, and the pleasures found in the thrills of criminality and the occasional riches that it can yield all influence why street children often remain on the street, rather than seek out alternative accommodation. A study of the psychological characteristics of South African street children concluded that street children describe freedom as their goal and highest value. The scope of this freedom is broad and has been described by researchers as,

> ... freedom from institutions, freedom of movement, freedom to choose activities and daily rhythms, and freedom from commitments ... The emotional sacrifice entailed in achieving these freedoms may be high and the value placed on them may, in part, be a defensive denial of that cost.

The challenge that social care providers face is to run shelters and educational programming that recognize the high value that street children place on freedom in the form of negative liberty, while providing them with new ways of conceptualizing and experiencing freedom through capabilities development in pursuit of positive liberties such as their intellectual, artistic, and vocational skills development.

Street children show their adaptive preferences when participating in art projects, and drawing images of their life aspirations which are often limited to the immediate employment opportunities around them such as selling fruits and vegetables and washing cars. Their experiences of stigma can cause street children to internalize the negative perceptions that members of the public have of them and to exhibit anti-social and self-destructive behaviour through joining gangs and/or engaging in crime. Erik Erikson explains the psychological process by which an individual or group that has been stigmatized may manifest self-destructive behaviour and develop perverse preferences. He states that they become delinquents and dropouts and invest 'pride, as well as need for total orientation in becoming exactly what the careless community expects them to become.'

Nussbaum describes the adaptive preferences of impoverished Indian women who lived in dirty living quarters and suffered from food insecurity:

> Before the arrival of the government consciousness-raising program, these women apparently had no feeling of anger or protest about their physical situation . . . They did not consider their conditions unhealthful or unsanitary, and they did not consider themselves to be malnourished. The consciousness-raising program has clearly challenged entrenched preferences and satisfactions.

Similarly, without government intervention street children are unlikely to realize just how much their mental and physical health is suffering as a result of their living on the street. They become so used to the street that eventually they too know no other way, and they become acclimated to poor living conditions because that is all that the street has ever provided them. (And because the homes that they ran away from rarely provided them with their needs either.) Just as the impoverished Indian women that Nussbaum interviewed only came to challenge the poverty of their living conditions when their consciousness was raised, so too, street children will only recognize that the street is not conducive to their healthy maturation and does not provide them with their human rights when they are the beneficiaries of similar consciousness raising programs. Nussbaum states that the results of such consciousness raising outreach programs have been successful at addressing harmful adaptive preferences. ". . . In case after case, we see women quickly dropping habituated preferences and adjusting their preferences in accordance with a new sense of their dignity and equality."

Some street children suffer from 'learned helplessness,' an attitude that emerges from experiences of powerlessness and lack of control over one's environment, and a history of repeated failures of attempting to exercise control over one's life. It entails the expression of an accepting attitude to street life, and a lack of interest and energy to pursue alternatives to it. For example, a child living on the street may give up attempting to find alternatives to the street after having been intimidated and mocked by his peers when expressing a desire to leave the street, or after being threatened by an adult that exploits him to engage in criminal activities or prostitution, who wants him to remain on the street to continue to carry out those activities.

Street children have difficulty imagining other opportunities beyond the street; frequently they do not have access to information about alternative accommodation for disadvantaged children and youth. There are insufficient numbers of social workers on the street teaching street children about their options, and helping them to leave the street. Street children often lack the capacity to make an appropriate risk assessment regarding the nature of their behaviour on the street, and their choice of the street as a permanent dwelling. Furthermore, street children often have difficulty understanding that the choices that they make as children and youth will have long term effects on their future employability, educational qualifications, and ability to socialize into society and enjoy society's benefits. They may, for example indicate the desire to become professionals and work in jobs such as law, teaching, or medicine—but often they are not aware that it is virtually impossible to achieve such goals without formal education and a stable and settled living situation.

Every child living on the street should be encouraged to voluntarily leave the street and move to a shelter for street children. For those children that refuse such an opportunity, the government should place them in residential care, paying careful attention not to separate siblings from one another. The quality of residential care for street children needs to be improved so that shelters are more appealing to street children and so that they are equipped to meet the full range of street children's needs. At present, too many shelters in the developing world are understaffed and have inadequate facilities. The love and relational needs of children need to be given far greater attention than they currently receive in residential care facilities. Programs for street children in which adult volunteers serve as mentors need to be established, so that street children can form close, supportive relationships with adults. . . .

Governments Should Help Children Leave the Street

Although living conditions on the street are poor, and morbidity rates of street children extremely high, there is still hesitation on the part of government agencies to take children off the street and place them in a more stable and secure living environment. This generally cautious attitude is in part, appropriate. Certain forms of coercion are highly ineffective and often entail the violations of the human rights of street children. But, recognition that such forms of coercion are neither ethical because of their failure to respect children, nor effective, because the children almost always return to the streets when aggressively forced into shelters, does not absolve the government of its responsibility to realize the human rights of children. The concern of government agencies to avoid coercion of street children is justified. But it also leads to inertia and a misunderstanding of the difference between legally sanctioned, and even legally required coercion (such as ensuring that children attend school and live in a safe environment), with forms of coercion that are illegal and morally reprehensible, such as arbitrary arrest and detention. These forms of coercion should not be conflated, and it is equally essential that the former be accepted, and the latter rejected.

There is a significant academic literature that, while claiming not to romanticize the street, in effect, does so. It focuses on the capacity of street children to survive on the street in the short term, showing little care for their-long term development and the negative psychological and physical health consequences of street life. It portrays them as being able to develop a sense of dignity and self-esteem in a context that is indifferent at best and, more commonly, hostile and retarding of development. It does not define a minimal criteria for freedom, ignoring their social and economic rights, particularly those to formal educational schooling and safe accommodation by arguing for the acceptability of the street, instead of challenging the government agencies that are responsible for their well-being to insure that street children, like all children, have access to schooling and social support.

Allowing children to live on the street does not show respect for their preferences, rather, it shows a lack of appreciation for the harsh reality of their lives. Their 'preferences' are typically adaptive and deformed—they are largely predetermined by the structural deprivations and pathologies of street life and thus the 'choices' that they make cannot be considered to be choices made under conditions of freedom. Moreover, their decisions are harmful to their own well-being and prevent them from acquiring the capabilities that Nussbaum shows are so essential for healthy human development. The right to life is a child's most fundamental right. Anything that threatens this primary right, the right upon which all other rights are based and without which they are meaningless—must be vigorously combated. The street undermines this right, and street children require the assistance of the government to help them leave the street, and to find a living and learning environment that will allow them to develop as genuinely free human beings that are capable of enjoying freedom and exercising autonomy.

"*Almost half the runaways calling the [National Runaway Switchboard] say family conflict is the reason they left home.*"

Teens Run Away for Many Reasons

Julie Mehta

There are many reasons why teens run away from home. Family conflict, however, is the most common cause, maintains Julie Mehta in the following excerpt. Because living on the street can expose teens to significant dangers, teens contemplating leaving home should seek out resources such as the National Runaway Switchboard to help them explore their options, the author recommends. Julie Mehta is a writer who has contributed to Current Health 2, *a* Weekly Reader *publication.*

As you read, consider the following questions:

1. What are some of the dangers facing street teens that the author cites?

2. What are some of the conflicts within a family that can cause teens to run away, according to the author?

3. What three questions should teens contemplating running away ask themselves, according to the head of the National Runaway Switchboard, as quoted by Mehta?

The first time Maria ran away, she didn't bring anything with her. "I wanted to be free and independent," says 15-year-old Maria, who admits she was "hanging out with the wrong people." Maria's mother didn't want her daughter going to parties and had just taken away her phone. So Maria cut school with a friend who had previously run away; they thought they would stay at someone's house for the night.

Instead, they ended up on the streets of a dangerous neighborhood in San Francisco. "It felt unsafe," says Maria. "There was lots of drug use and prostitution." After three days, Maria returned home because she missed her family. But she ran away again and again. "I always thought I'd be staying with another person, but I always ended up on the street," she says.

Why would teens like Maria give up the comforts of home for uncertainty and danger? "It's rarely just one thing," says Maureen Blaha, executive director of the National Runaway Switchboard (NRS), of the reasons that teens sometimes run away. "It's been building up, and they think anything is better than home." But even if things are bad at home, life on the street could be much worse.

What Can Go Wrong

One risk of running away is finding yourself with no place to sleep. Many runaway youths actually do manage to stay with relatives or friends at first. They may attempt what's called "couch surfing"—going from one friend's house to another night after night. But eventually, they'll probably have to hit the road and search for a shelter or another place to crash. Studies show that 12 percent of runaway and homeless youths have spent at least one night sleeping outside—on a park bench, under a bridge, or on a rooftop.

Finding a bed is just one of many challenges runaway teens face. They live in danger of being robbed or attacked. A study of teen runaways in the Midwest found that more than 20 percent had been beaten up multiple times, and more than a quarter had been robbed.

Any food and money that runaways manage to save or acquire quickly runs out, and hunger often provokes desperate measures. "When kids run from home, initially they are very vulnerable to perpetrators and often become victims of crime," says Blaha. "After a while, in order to survive, they become the perpetrators. So they may be hungry and go into a convenience store and steal something to eat, or they may be cold and will do whatever it takes in order to have a place to sleep."

Another big problem for runaway teens is substance abuse. The study of midwestern runaways found that roughly two-thirds had used alcohol and marijuana, and more than 20 percent had tried methamphetamines and hallucinogenic drugs. Runaways may think drugs will help numb the grim realities of their lives.

Who Runs?

You may know someone who has risked these hazards by running away. Between 1.6 million and 2.8 million youths run away each year, according to studies cited on the NRS Web site. And while 57 percent of runaways who call NRS have been away from home less than a week, 24 percent have been away as long as a month and 3 percent longer than six months.

Almost half the runaways calling the switchboard say family conflict is the reason they left home. "Typically this is not just a child problem—it's a family problem," says Ted Feinberg, assistant executive director of the National Association of School Psychologists. Situations such as divorce and new stepparents can make the roller-coaster ride of adolescence feel even more turbulent.

For 15-year-old Kev, the problems started long before he ran away. He'd had conflicts with his stepdad for years, especially after his half brother and half sister were born. "I know a lot of kids who've run away," Kev says, "and it's usually because they don't feel loved at home. I used to get all the attention."

The tension escalated when Kev fell in love with a girl his stepdad didn't like. "My mouth often gets me into trouble," the Pennsylvania teen admits. He'd been grounded for two weeks with no phone or TV privileges. Then he got a call from his girlfriend, and his stepdad "flipped out." Kev left home and ended up at a shelter.

Other teens run away because they fear telling their parents about a pregnancy or revealing they are gay. Causes that don't involve family can include a recent breakup, difficulties at school, substance abuse, or mental health issues such as depression. In rare cases, teens may even be lured away by someone they met online, realizing too late that the person is not what he or she claimed to be.

Fleeing from Pain

It's easy to look at the examples above and assume that runaways should just work out their problems with their families. But in other cases, talking things out isn't the answer—teens are actually in danger. Some young people run away from homes where they face abuse, neglect, or family members battling their own drug or alcohol problems.

The trouble began for 17-year-old Ryan when he was a toddler and his mentally ill father took off. Ryan's mother became addicted to crystal meth and physically abused him. Social services eventually placed the Arizona teen with his uncles in Nevada, but the abuse continued there.

One day he decided to leave his uncles and go back to his mom, despite knowing she was still on drugs. "I had school and football practice in the morning, and I just got on the bus and went back to Arizona," Ryan remembers. But once he got there, "things went even more downhill."

Ryan stayed with his mother at a hotel until she was arrested; then he had nowhere to go. He slept in his mom's car until he sold it for bus fare back to Nevada. Now he lives at a group home, is back in school, and has a job.

Ryan suggests that teens in similar situations look for help from local agencies before trying to escape on their own. "The principal always knows something about where to get help. Even a teacher. Ask people you like and trust. You could even get [Child Protective Services] involved. Don't give up trying to get help."

Resist the Road

Before running, Blaha suggests, teens should stop and ask themselves three questions:

1. Is there anything I can do to change the situation?

2. What would need to change in order for me to stay home?

3. How will I survive if I run away?

She encourages teens to call the NRS before they decide to leave. "We have 16,000 resources in our database," Blaha says. "We can help them develop a plan of action."

Callers talk to volunteers such as Amanda Hetherington, 17, who's answered more than a hundred calls at NRS headquarters in Chicago. She says teens who call often feel they aren't being heard: "We talk about their support system. Sometimes they'll have an aunt or grandma who can serve as a go-between. . . . Sometimes a friend can help. Or maybe they can try getting involved in extra curriculars. . . . Usually there's at least one thing they haven't thought of."

If teens decide to leave home, the door isn't always closed behind them. For Maria, staying at a group home for a while helped her realize the love she had at her real home. She's returned to her family, stopped running away, and is trying to rebuild relationships with old friends.

A Different Path

If you have a friend who's talking about running, you can help make him or her think twice. "You aren't doing your friend or yourself a favor in keeping quiet in a situation that could be dangerous. You have to let an adult know," says Feinberg. "You can maybe say, 'I'll go with you to the counselor if you're nervous.'"

Kev's best friend ran away because of a conflict with his own stepdad. When the friend returned home, Kev went with him for moral support. As for Kev, he and his mother decided it would be a good idea for him to live with an uncle for a while.

"Running away is not the best thing to do. You'll fall behind in school and may end up dropping out," Kev says. "I have things I want to do, like every kid. It will take some time, but I know I will turn my life around."

> "It is clear that LGBT youth experience homelessness at a disproportionate rate."

Gay and Transgender Teens Are at Increased Risk of Becoming Street Teens

Nicholas Ray

Nicholas Ray is senior policy analyst for the National Gay and Lesbian Task Force.

Lesbian, gay, bisexual, and transgender (LGBT) youth make up a much higher percentage of all homeless youth than their proportion of the US population, according to this viewpoint by Nicholas Ray. The reason LGBT youth are more likely to become homeless than their heterosexual peers has to do with the issue of family conflict. Family conflict is the major reason kids become homeless, and half of the teens coming out as gay received a negative parental reaction, according to Ray. Once LGBT youth are on the street, they are more likely to engage in behaviors that threaten their well-being.

Nicholas Ray, "Executive Summary," *Lesbian, Gay, Bisexual and Transgender Youth: An Epidemic of Homelessness*. New York: National Gay and Lesbian Task Force Policy Institute and the National Coalition for the Homeless, 2006, pp. 1–7. Copyright © 2006 by the National Gay and Lesbian Task Force. All rights reserved. Reproduced by permission.

As you read, consider the following questions:

1. Why do homeless youth engage in risky sexual behaviors, according to the author?

2. What are some of the problems cited by the author that LGBT teens face when they seek out shelters?

3. What policy recommendations at the federal level does the author make?

The U.S. Department of Health and Human Services estimates that the number of homeless and runaway youth ranges from 575,000 to 1.6 million per year. Our [the National Gay and Lesbian Task Force with the National Coalition for the Homeless] analysis of the available research suggests that between 20 percent and 40 percent of all homeless youth identify as lesbian, gay, bisexual or transgender (LGBT). Given that between 3 percent and 5 percent of the U.S. population identifies as lesbian, gay or bisexual, it is clear that LGBT youth experience homelessness at a disproportionate rate....

Why LGBT Youth Become Homeless

Family conflict is the primary cause of homelessness for all youth, LGBT or straight. Specifically, familial conflict over a youth's sexual orientation or gender identity is a significant factor that leads to homelessness or the need for out-of-home care. According to one study, 50 percent of gay teens experienced a negative reaction from their parents when they came out and 26 percent were kicked out of their homes. Another study found that more than one-third of youth who are homeless or in the care of social services experienced a violent physical assault when they came out, which can lead to youth leaving a shelter or foster home because they actually feel safer on the streets.

Homelessness Presents Dangers to LGBT Youth

Whether LGBT youth are homeless on the streets or in temporary shelter, our review of the available research reveals that they face a multitude of ongoing crises that threaten their chances of becoming healthy, independent adults.

LGBT homeless youth are especially vulnerable to depression, loneliness and psychosomatic illness, withdrawn behavior, social problems and delinquency. According to the U.S. Department of Health and Human Services, the fact that LGBT youth live in "a society that discriminates against and stigmatizes homosexuals" makes them more vulnerable to mental health issues than heterosexual youth. This vulnerability is only magnified for LGBT youth who are homeless.

The combination of stressors inherent to the daily life of homeless youth leads them to abuse drugs and alcohol. For example, in Minnesota, five separate statewide studies found that between 10 and 20 percent of homeless youth self-identify as chemically dependent. These risks are exacerbated for homeless youth identifying as lesbian, gay or bisexual (LGB). Personal drug usage, family drug usage, and the likelihood of enrolling in a treatment program are all higher for LGB homeless youth than for their heterosexual peers.

All homeless youth are especially vulnerable to engaging in risky sexual behaviors because their basic needs for food and shelter are not being met. Defined as "exchanging sex for anything needed, including money, food, clothes, a place to stay or drugs," survival sex is the last resort for many LGBT homeless youth. A study of homeless youth in Canada found that those who identify as LGBT were three times more likely to participate in survival sex than their heterosexual peers, and 50 percent of homeless youth in another study considered it likely or very likely that they will someday test positive for HIV.

Hollywood Is a Beacon for Homeless Gays

The city hipsters sipping expensive coffee and chatting on cellphones did not give a second look at the two young men cutting across a Hollywood courtyard on their way to bed down in a nearby park.

AJ, 23, and his boyfriend, Alex, 21, hide their blankets and duffel bags in bushes. They shower every morning at a drop-in center and pick out outfits from a closet full of used yet youthful attire.

"If I could be invisible, I would," AJ said. "I feel ashamed to admit that I'm homeless."

Alexandra Zavis, "Gay and Homeless: In Plain Sight, a Largely Hidden Population," Los Angeles Times, December 12, 2010.

LGBT youth face the threat of victimization everywhere: at home, at school, at their jobs, and, for those who are out-of-home, at shelters and on the streets. According to the National Runaway Switchboard, LGBT homeless youth are seven times more likely than their heterosexual peers to be victims of a crime. While some public safety agencies try to help this vulnerable population, others adopt a "blame the victim" approach, further decreasing the odds of victimized youth feeling safe reporting their experiences.

While there is a paucity of academic research about the experiences of LGBT youth who end up in the juvenile and criminal justice systems, preliminary evidence suggests that they are disproportionately the victims of harassment and violence, including rape. For example, respondents in one small study reported that lesbians and bisexual girls are overrepresented in the juvenile justice system and that they are forced to live among a population of inmates who are violently homophobic. Gay male youth in the system are also emotionally, physically and sexually assaulted by staff and inmates. One respondent in a study of the legal rights of young people in state custody reported that staff members think that "[if] a youth is gay, they want to have sex with all the other boys, so they did not protect me from unwanted sexual advances."

Transgender youth are disproportionately represented in the homeless population. More generally, some reports indicate that one in five transgender individuals need or are at risk of needing homeless shelter assistance. However, most shelters are segregated by birth sex, regardless of the individual's gender identity, and homeless transgender youth are even ostracized by some agencies that serve their LGB peers.

Homelessness Programs Have Problems

Since 1974, when the federal government enacted the original Runaway Youth Act, there have been numerous pieces of legislation addressing youth homelessness. Most recently, the Runaway, Homeless and Missing Children Protection Act (RHMCPA) was signed into law by President George W. Bush in 2003 and is up for reauthorization in 2008.

Among the most important provisions of this complex piece of legislation are programs that allocate funding for core homeless youth services, including basic drop-in centers, street outreach efforts, transitional living programs (TLPs) and the National Runaway Switchboard. While the law does not allocate funding for LGBT-specific services, some funds have been awarded to agencies who work exclusively with LGBT youth, as well as those who seek to serve LGBT homeless youth as part of a broader mission.

Unfortunately, homeless youth programs have been grossly under funded, contributing to a shortfall of available spaces for youth who need support. In 2004 alone, due to this lack of funding, more than 2,500 youth were denied access to a TLP program for which they were otherwise qualified. Additionally, 4,200 youth were turned away from Basic Center Programs, which provide family reunification services and emergency shelter.

Lack of funding is not the only obstacle preventing LGBT homeless youth from receiving the services they need. In 2002, President George W. Bush issued an executive order permitting federal funding for faith-based organizations (FBOs) to provide social services. While more and more FBOs are receiving federal funds, overall funding levels for homeless youth services have not increased. Consequently, there is a possibility that the impact of FBOs will not be to increase services to the homeless, but rather only to change *who* provides those services.

A number of faith-based providers oppose legal and social equality for LGBT people, which raises serious questions about whether LGBT homeless youth can access services in a safe and nurturing environment. If an organization's core belief is that homosexuality is wrong, that organization (and its committed leaders and volunteers) may not respect a client's sexual orientation or gender identity and may expose LGBT youth to discriminatory treatment. . . .

LGBT Youth Are Mistreated in Shelters

The majority of existing shelters and other care systems are not providing safe and effective services to LGBT homeless youth. For example, in New York City, more than 60 percent of beds for homeless youth are provided by Covenant House, a facility where LGBT youth report that they have been threatened, belittled and abused by staff and other youth because of their sexual orientation or gender identity.

At one residential placement facility in Michigan, LGBT teens, or those suspected of being LGBT, were forced to wear orange jumpsuits to alert staff and other residents. At another transitional housing placement, staff removed the bedroom door of an out gay youth, supposedly to ward off any homosexual behavior. The second bed in the room was left empty and other residents were warned that if they misbehaved they would have to share the room with the "gay kid."

LGBT homeless youth at the Home for Little Wanderers in Massachusetts have reported being kicked out of other agencies when they revealed their sexual orientation or gender identity. Many also said that the risks inherent to living in a space that was not protecting them made them think that they were better off having unsafe sex and contracting HIV because they would then be eligible for specific housing funds reserved for HIV-positive homeless people in need.

Despite the potential for mistreatment of LGBT homeless youth by some agencies, there are others who set an example for their peers. Our [research focuses on] five contributing homeless youth service providers represent the diverse range of agencies working with homeless LGBT youth, though they are by no means the only agencies doing great work. . . .

Change Is Possible

This report concludes with a series of policy recommendations that can help to curb the epidemic of LGBT youth homelessness. While our focus in this publication and in these policy recommendations is to address LGBT-specific concerns, we believe that homelessness is not an issue that can be tackled piecemeal. Wholesale improvement is needed, and that is what we propose. Our recommendations are not intended to be an exhaustive list of every policy change that would make the experience of homeless youth better. Rather, we highlight some of the crucial problem areas where policy change is both needed and reasonably possible.

Federal Level Recommendations:

1. Reauthorize and increase appropriations for federal Runaway and Homeless Youth Act (RHYA) programs.

2. Permit youth who are minors, especially unaccompanied minors, to receive primary and specialty health care services without the consent of a parent or guardian.

3. Develop a national estimate of the incidence and prevalence of homelessness among American youth, gathering data that aids in the provision of appropriate services.

4. Authorize and appropriate federal funds for developmental, preventive and intervention programs targeted to LGBT youth.

5. Raise federal and state minimum wages to an appropriate level.

6. Broaden the U.S. Department of Housing and Urban Development's definition of "homeless individual" to include living arrangements common to homeless youth.

State and Local Level Recommendations:

1. Establish funding streams to provide housing options for all homeless youth. Require that recipients of these funds are committed to the safe and appropriate treatment of LGBT homeless youth, with penalties for non-compliance including the loss of government funding. These funds would supplement federal appropriations.

2. Permit dedicated shelter space and housing for LGBT youth.

3. Repeal existing laws and policies that prevent single and partnered LGBT individuals from serving as adoptive and foster parents.

4. Discourage the criminalization of homelessness and the activities inherent to the daily lives of people experiencing homelessness.

5. Expand the availability of comprehensive health insurance and services to all low-income youth through the age of 24 via Medicaid.

Practitioner Level Recommendations:

1. Require all agencies that seek government funding and licensure to serve homeless youth to demonstrate awareness and cultural competency of LGBT issues and populations at the institutional level and to adopt nondiscrimination policies for LGBT youth.

2. Mandate individual-level LGBT awareness training and demonstrated cultural competency as a part of the professional licensing process of all health and social service professions.

3. Mandate LGBT awareness training for all state agency staff who work in child welfare or juvenile justice divisions.

Once implemented, these policy recommendations will help not only LGBT homeless youth, but all youth abandoned by their family or forced to leave home. In this report, we extensively review the academic and professional literature on the myriad challenges faced by LGBT homeless youth. The research shows that despite these challenges, many of these youth are remarkably resilient and have benefited from support from agencies like those in our model programs chapters who have worked to ensure that youth feel safe, welcome and supported. Regardless of sexual orientation or gender identity, every young person deserves a safe and nurturing environment in which to grow and learn. It is our hope that this report will bring renewed attention to an issue that has been inadequately addressed for far too long.

> *"An increasing number of children [are leaving] home for life on the streets. . . . Foreclosures, layoffs, rising food and fuel prices, and inadequate supplies of low-cost housing have stretched families to the extreme."*

Kids Are Running Away Because of the Bad Economy

Ian Urbina

Ian Urbina is a reporter for the New York Times.

There has been an increase in the number of youth running away from home since 2008, and the recession is to blame for the surge, Urbina maintains in the following viewpoint. Families are facing increasing economic pressure and the stress this creates can exacerbate family conflict. In some cases, children become throwaway youth when their parents tell them they can no longer afford to support them.

As you read, consider the following questions:

1. What statistic does the author cite to support his claim of the growth in homelessness among juveniles?

2. Why don't some parents report their children as missing, according to the author?

3. What reasons do police officials give for not reporting names of missing youth to the National Center for Missing and Exploited Children?

Dressed in soaked green pajamas, Betty Snyder, 14, huddled under a cold drizzle at the city park as several older boys decided what to do with her.

Betty said she had run away from home a week earlier after a violent argument with her mother. Shivering and sullen-faced, she vowed that she was not going to sleep by herself again behind the hedges downtown, where older homeless men and methamphetamine addicts might find her.

The boys were also runaways. But unlike them, Betty said, she had been reported missing to the police. That meant that if the boys let her stay overnight in their hidden tent encampment by the freeway, they risked being arrested for harboring a fugitive.

"We keep running into this," said one of the boys, Clinton Anchors, 18. Over the past year, he said, he and five other teenagers living together on the streets had taken under their wings no fewer than 20 children—some as young as 12—and taught them how to avoid predators and the police, survive the cold and find food.

"We always first try to send them home," said Clinton, who himself ran away from home at 12. "But a lot of times they won't go, because things are really bad there. We basically become their new family."

The Recession Causes More Children to Leave Home

Over the past two years [since October 2009], government officials and experts have seen an increasing number of children leave home for life on the streets, including many under 13.

Foreclosures, layoffs, rising food and fuel prices and inadequate supplies of low-cost housing have stretched families to the extreme, and those pressures have trickled down to teenagers and preteens.

Federal studies and experts in the field have estimated that at least 1.6 million juveniles run away or are thrown out of their homes annually. But most of those return home within a week, and the government does not conduct a comprehensive or current count.

The best measure of the problem may be the number of contacts with runaways that federally-financed outreach programs make, which rose to 761,000 in 2008 from 550,000 in 2002, when current methods of counting began. (The number fell in 2007, but rose sharply again last year, and the number of federal outreach programs has been fairly steady throughout the period.)

Too young to get a hotel room, sign a lease or in many cases hold a job, young runaways are increasingly surviving by selling drugs, panhandling or engaging in prostitution, according to the National Runaway Switchboard, the federally-financed national hot line created in 1974. Legitimate employment was hard to find in the summer of 2009; the Labor Department said fewer than 30 percent of teenagers had jobs.

In more than 50 interviews over 11 months, teenagers living on their own in eight states told of a harrowing existence that in many cases involved sleeping in abandoned buildings, couch-surfing among friends and relatives or camping on riverbanks and in parks after fleeing or being kicked out by families in financial crisis.

The runaways spend much of their time avoiding the authorities because they assume the officials are trying to send them home. But most often the police are not looking for them as missing-person cases at all, just responding to complaints about loitering or menacing. In fact, federal data indicate that usually no one is looking for the runaways, either because parents have not reported them missing or the police have mishandled the reports. . . .

Between Legal and Illegal

Survival on the streets of Medford, a city of 76,000 in southwest Oregon, requires runaways to walk a fine line between legal and illegal activity, as a few days with a group of them showed. Even as they sought help from social service organizations, they guarded their freedom jealously.

Petulant and street savvy, they were children nonetheless. One girl said she used a butter knife and a library card to break into vacant houses. But after she began living in one of them, she ate dry cereal for dinner for weeks because she did not realize that she could use the microwave to boil water for Ramen noodles. Another girl was childlike enough to suck her thumb, but dangerous enough to carry a switchblade.

They camped in restricted areas, occasionally shoplifted and regularly smoked marijuana. But they stayed away from harder drugs or drug dealing, and the older teenagers fiercely protected the younger runaways from sexual or other physical threats.

In waking hours, members of the group split their time among a park, a pool hall and a video-game arcade, sharing cigarettes. When in need, they sometimes barter: a sleeveless jacket for a blanket, peanut butter for extra lighter fluid to start campfires on soggy nights.

Betty Snyder, the newcomer in the park, said she had bitten her mother in a recent fight. She said she often refused to do household chores, which prompted heated arguments.

"I'm just tired of it all, and I don't want to be in my house anymore," she said, explaining why she had run away. "One month there is money, and the next month there is none. One day, she is taking it out on me and hitting me, and the next day she is ignoring me. It's more stable out here."

Members of the group said they sometimes made money by picking parking meters or sitting in front of parking lots, pretending to be the attendant after the real one leaves. When things get really desperate, they said, they climb into public fountains to fish out coins late at night. On cold nights, they hide in public libraries or schools after closing time to sleep.

Many of the runaways said they had fled family conflicts or the strain of their parents' alcohol or drug abuse. Others said they left simply because they did not want to go to school or live by their parents' rules.

"I can survive fine out here," Betty said as she brandished a switchblade she pulled from her dirty sweatshirt pocket. At a nearby picnic table was part of the world she and the others were trying to avoid: a man with swastikas tattooed on his neck and an older homeless woman with rotted teeth, holding a pit bull named Diablo.

But Betty and another 14-year-old, seeming not to notice, went off to play on a park swing. Around the country, outreach workers and city officials say they have been overwhelmed with requests for help from young people in desperate straits. . . .

"Several times a month we're seeing kids being left by parents who say they can't afford them anymore," said Mary Ferrell, director of the Maslow Project, a resource center for homeless children and families in Medford. With fewer jobs available, teenagers are less able to help their families financially. Relatives and family friends are less likely to take them in.

While federal officials say homelessness overall is expected to rise 10 percent to 20 percent this year, a federal survey of schools showed a 40 percent increase in the number of juveniles living on their own last year, more than double the number in 2003. . . .

Traveling Alone

Maureen Blaha, executive director of the National Runaway Switchboard, said that while most runaways, like those in Medford, opt to stay in their hometowns, some venture farther away and face greater dangers. The farther they get from home and the longer they stay out, the less money they have and the more likely they are to take risks with people they have just met, Ms. Blaha said.

"A lot of small-town kids figure they can go to Chicago, San Francisco or New York because they can disappear there," she said.

Martin Jaycard, a Port Authority police officer in New York, sees himself as a last line of defense in preventing that from happening.

Dressed in scraggly blue jeans and an untucked open-collar shirt, Officer Jaycard, a seven-year police veteran, is part of the Port Authority's Youth Services Unit. His job is to catch runaways as they pass through the Port Authority Bus Terminal, the nation's busiest.

"You're the last person these kids want to see," he said, estimating that his three-officer unit stops at least one runaway a day at the terminal.

Invisible Names

Lacking the training or the expertise to spot runaways, most police officers would not have stopped [a] girl waiting for the bus. Even if they had, her name probably would not have been listed in the federal database called the National Crime Information Center, or N.C.I.C., which among other things tracks missing people.

Federal statistics indicate that in more than three-quarters of runaway cases, parents or caretakers have not reported the child missing, often because they are angry about a fight or would simply prefer to see a problem child leave the house.

Experts say some parents fear that involving the police will get them or their children into trouble or put their custody at risk.

And in 16 percent of cases, the local police failed to enter the information into the federal database, as required under federal law, according to a review of federal data by *The New York Times*.

Among the 61,452 names that were reported to the National Center for Missing and Exploited Children from January 2004 to January 2009, there were about 9,625 instances involving children whose missing-persons reports were not entered into the N.C.I.C., according to the review by *The Times*. If the names are not in the national database, then only local police agencies know whom to look for.

Police officials give various reasons for not entering the data. The software is old and cumbersome, they say, or they have limited resources and need to prioritize their time. In many cases, the police said, they do not take runaway reports as seriously as abductions, in part because runaways are often fleeing family problems. The police also say that entering every report into the federal database could make a city's situation appear to be more of a problem than it is.

But in 267 of the cases around the nation for which the police did not enter a report into the database, the children remain missing. In 58, they were found dead.

"If no one knows they're gone, who is going to look for them?" said Tray Williams, a spokesman for the Louisiana Office of Child Services, whose job it was to take care of 17-year-old Cleveland Randall.

On Feb. 6, Cleveland ran away from his foster care center in New Orleans and took a bus to Mississippi. His social workers reported him missing, but the New Orleans police failed to enter the report into the N.C.I.C. Ten days later, Cleveland was found shot to death in Avondale, La.

"These kids might as well be invisible if they aren't in N.C.I.C.," said Ernie Allen, the director of the National Center for Missing and Exploited Children.

Paradise by Interstate 5

Invisibility, many of the runaways in Medford say, is just what they want.

By midnight, the group decided it was late enough for them to leave the pool hall and to move around the city discreetly. So they went their separate ways.

Alex Molnar, 18, took the back alleys to a 24-hour laundry to sleep under the folding tables. If people were still using the machines, he planned on locking himself in the restroom, placing a sign on the front saying "Out of Service."

On the other side of the city, Alex Hughes, 16, took side streets to a secret clearing along Interstate 5.

On colder nights, he and Clinton Anchors have built a fire in a long shallow trench, eventually covering it with dirt to create a heated mound where they could put their blankets.

Building a lean-to with a tarp and sticks, Clinton lifted his voice above the roar of the tractor-trailers barreling by just feet away. He said they called the spot "paradise" because the police rarely checked for them there.

"Even if they do, Betty is not with us, so that's good," he added, explaining that she had found a friend willing to lend her couch for the night. "One less thing to worry about."

Periodical and Internet Sources Bibliography

The following articles have been selected to supplement the diverse views presented in this chapter.

ABC News	"Teen Lovers Talk About Life on the Lam," January 23, 2008, Abcnews.go.com.
Justeen Hyde	"From Home to Street: Understanding Young People's Transitions into Homelessness," *Journal of Adolescence*, vol. 28, no. 2, 2005, pp. 171–83.
Janet Kornblum	"Runaway Runs Back," *USA Today*, February 27, 2008, p. ID.
Rich Lombino and Elizabeth Lombino	"Don't Forget, Runaway Teens Are Homeless, Too," Change.org, June 4, 2010, Uspoverty.change.org/blog.
Claudine Martijn and Louise Sharpe	"Pathways to Youth Homelessness," *Social Science & Medicine*, vol. 62, 2006, pp. 1–12.
Susan Payne	"Runaway Youth and Troubled Teens Are Serious Social Issues," Suite101.com, February 10, 2010. www.suite101.com.
Rebecca P. Sanchez, Martha W. Waller, and Jody M. Greene	"Who Runs? A Demographic Profile of Runaway Youth in the United States," *Journal of Adolescent Health*, vol. 39, no. 5, 2006, pp. 778–81.
Esther Usborne, John E. Lydon, and Donald M. Taylor	"Goals and Social Relationships: Windows into the Motivation and Well-Being of 'Street Kids,'" *Journal of Applied Social Psychology*, vol. 39, no. 5, 2009, pp. 1057–82.

What Are the Consequences of Being a Street Teen?

Chapter Preface

While running away from home may conjure up romantic images like the story of Huckleberry Finn, the reality is far starker. Postings on "Runaway Lives," a web-based forum for runaways, show some of the grim realities of life on the streets. Signing herself "Still Have Nightmares," a young girl tells of living in abandoned buildings, scavenging for food. She eventually began selling drugs to get money, got raped twice, survived two attempts on her life, got pregnant and lost her child. Finally, she was arrested and returned to her family. She concludes, "I'm lucky to be alive."

Teens often run away from home to escape dangerous situations. However, the risks they face on the streets can be greater than those they are running from. Since the mid-1970s, life on the streets has become increasingly dangerous because of the prevalence of drugs and increased risk of sexual exploitation. According to the National Runaway Switchboard, 75 percent of runaways who have been away from home for more than two weeks become involved in theft, drugs, or pornography, and one-third of all teens on the streets will become prostitutes within forty-eight hours of leaving home. Gay and bisexual youth are at greater risk of becoming prostitutes than heterosexual youth. Additional dangers facing street children are hunger, sexually transmitted diseases, drug and alcohol abuse, robbery, pregnancy, and physical and sexual abuse.

Although the National Runaway Switchboard reports that the largest percentage of runaway youth rely on friends and relatives for help (73 percent in 2009), it also reports a growing incidence of more dangerous means of support. Since 2009, the number of youth resorting to panhandling to survive has grown by 228 percent, those turning to the sex industry has increased by 58 percent, those selling drugs by 54 percent, and those stealing by 22 percent. Every year approximately five thousand homeless youth die due to assault, drugs, illness, or suicide. The consequences of being a street teen are debated in the viewpoints in the following chapter.

> *"Runaway and thrownaway youth who actually become homeless . . . almost inevitably turn to prostitution at some point as a means to meet their basic necessities."*

Street Teens Often Turn to Prostitution to Survive

R. Barri Flowers

Street youth are far more likely to become prostitutes than those who find shelter with friends or family, according to R. Barri Flowers in the following viewpoint. Approximately one-third of homeless youths turn to prostitution to survive life on the streets. Once they become prostitutes, they run a high risk of being victimized by their clients and pimps, as well as others they encounter in the sex trade. R. Barri Flowers is a literary criminologist and mystery novelist who has written more than forty books.

As you read, consider the following questions:

1. According to a report the author cites, what is the correlation between previous sexual abuse and the chance of becoming a prostitute?

2. How are youths who turn to prostitution frequently victimized, according to the author?

3. Why do child pornographers target runaway and thrown-away youths, according to the author?

Most runaway and thrownaway youth who become homeless inevitably turn to survival sex and prostitution to make ends meet in a street life that often robs them of their youth and forces them into high-risk activities. The thriving sex-for-sale industry in the United States includes a high number of teenage (and even some preteen) and young adult prostitutes who sell their bodies to and for customers, pimps, pedophiles, pornographers, gang members, and other sexual exploiters. Prostituted youth thus become victims and offenders of sex crimes at once, subjecting them to dangerous and often unprotected sexual relations with frequent, anonymous, and known partners, placing them at risk for sexually transmitted infections, including HIV, other illnesses, and arrest. Furthermore, juvenile prostitutes are typically involved with other risky experiences detrimental to their physical and mental health and well-being, such as substance abuse, intravenous drug use, sharing dirty needles, and various delinquencies and criminality. Many prostituted youth have been the victims of sexual and physical abuse at home, both of which have been shown to be strong predictors of running away and prostitution involvement. Though law enforcement has cracked down more on teenage prostitution and those who solicit the sexual services of minors in recent years, runaway/thrownaway youth who have nowhere else to turn continue to find their way into the sex trade as homeless, detached from parents and family, while being amongst other youth who have found themselves headed down the same path. . . .

Most experts on teenage prostitution believe that runaway and thrownaway youth who actually become homeless (as opposed to staying with a family member or friend) almost inevitably turn to prostitution at some point as a means to meet their basic necessities and often as a result of the coercive powers of pimps and other child sexual exploiters. According to a National Center for Missing and Exploited Children report, as many as one out of three runaway and homeless youth become involved in street prostitution or survival sex; whereas more than three in four prostituted youth have reported running away from home on at least one occasion. In Ruth Dean and Melissa Thomson's study of teenage prostitution, they found that the majority of prostituted youth run away from home or substitute care.

Other researchers have also shown a strong correlation between runaways and prostitution. [Nancy] Walker found that two in three teenage prostitutes were runaways, with more than eight in ten presently or previously homeless. The Klass Kids Foundation reported that an estimated 55 percent of homeless female youth were actively involved in the sex trade industry as prostitutes. In Z.M. Lukman's study of runaway prostituted youth, nearly 78 percent were said to be more likely to become prostitution-involved than participants in other delinquent or criminal behavior. David Barrett posited that being a runaway was a more significant dynamic in youth involvement in the sex-for-sale industry than sexual abuse.

Entry into Prostitution

The pathway into the world of prostitution for runaway, thrownaway, and homeless youth often comes with little time to truly digest the implications of selling sex and its associations in the street subculture. Studies show that within thirty-six to forty-eight hours, and sometimes even sooner, after a youth becomes homeless, they will be solicited for sexual favors; persuaded, coerced, recruited, or abducted into prostitution and/or pornography by pimps, customers, gangs, pedophiles, or pornographers. In many cases, the sexual exploiter may pretend to be interested in helping or romancing the new street youth in order to charm and seduce the unsuspecting, naive victim into compliance. Other times, the runaway or thrownaway may be supplied with alcohol or drugs as part of the recruitment and laying the groundwork process. Most newly homeless youth, away on their own for the first time and frightened, are easy marks for those who would take advantage of their desperation and vulnerability.

Researchers have found that the longer runaway/ thrownaway youth are without a secure place to call home, the likelihood they will never return to their original home increases, as does the probability of becoming prostituted or otherwise victims of sexual exploitation. Staying homeless for thirty days has been shown to be the single greatest dynamic in leading street youth to become prostitution-involved. However, most homeless youth enter the sex trade much sooner. According to one study, after two weeks of being homeless, three out of four runaways will have participated in prostitution, child pornography, drug, or delinquent activities.

The average age of entrance into prostitution is fourteen, with the median age for prostituted youth 15.5 years. Many prostituted youth have been reported to be under the age of twelve and in some cases as young as nine years of age. The average age for girls to enter prostitution is twelve to fourteen; while for boys and transgender youth, the average age of becoming prostitution-involved is eleven to thirteen.

Most prostituted youth escape from or are forced to leave unsafe or dysfunctional home environments that often include such issues as physical and sexual child abuse, substance abuse, domestic violence, mental illness, and family discord. Many also have school or peer problems that play a role in their leaving home. Unfortunately, the street world they enter provides a host of new troubles, unstable living conditions, dangerous situations, exploiters and victimizers, and negative connotations that few, if any, homeless youth are equipped to deal with.

Prostituted Youth and Child Sexual Abuse

The relationship between child sexual abuse and prostituted youth has been well documented in the literature. One report noted that sexual abuse "has a significant impact on the probability that a runaway will become involved with prostitution," further suggesting that "sex abuse appears to indirectly increase the chance of prostitution by increasing the risk of running away."

Most runaway youth who enter prostitution have been victims of physical and sexual abuse, with the latter the strongest indicator of becoming drawn into the sex trade industry. Some studies report that more than half of runaway youth were victims of sexual and physical abuse. An Australian study found that nearly three out of four runaways had been sexual abuse victims prior to reaching the age of fourteen. Similarly, another study found that almost eight in ten prostituted girls had been victims of child molestation, and nine in ten victims of physical abuse before entrance into prostitution. In Stephen Gaetz's research, homeless street youth were said to be five times more likely than non homeless youth to have been sexually abused while living at home. . . .

Violence Encountered by Prostituted Youth

Prostitution-involved youth are frequently the targets of violence perpetrated by customers, pimps, pedophiles, pornographers, gangs, and others they encounter in the sex trade and street life. The victimization is in the form of physical assaults, rape/sexual assaults, forced sexual perversions, robberies, verbal attacks, intimidation, and other violence, including murder. As most underage prostitutes are neither physically nor mentally equipped to defend themselves against attackers, while being in a high-risk environment for violence, they face potential threats to their health and well-being at every turn. According to studies, around two in three prostituted youth are the victims of violence perpetrated by pimps and custom-

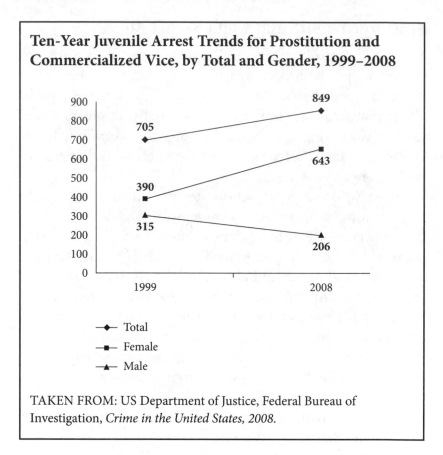

Ten-Year Juvenile Arrest Trends for Prostitution and Commercialized Vice, by Total and Gender, 1999–2008

TAKEN FROM: US Department of Justice, Federal Bureau of Investigation, *Crime in the United States, 2008.*

ers. Another study of street prostitutes found a high rate of rape and other violence in the course of prostituting.

Prostituted female youth tend to be the victims of sexual assaults more often than prostituted male youth in the street environment, given their greater association with pimps and physically superior violent Johns and other victimizers. However, boy prostitutes are still vulnerable to sexual and physical assaults by older males, gang members, and others who prey on children. One study found that prostituted males tended to be victimized through assaults and robberies most often by "homophobic male onlookers" than customers.

All young prostitutes are at risk of being murdered. Apart from the everyday threats of potential fatal violence from customers, pimps, and drug addicts prostituted youth face, they are also a prime target of sexual and serial killers. For instance, the so-called Green River Killer murdered at least forty-eight females during the 1980s and 1990s in Washington and Oregon. Most of the victims were runaways and teenage prostitutes.

Though prostitution-involved youth are prone to every type of violence that exists in the homeless world, most shy away from reporting their victimization to the authorities for fear of being disregarded, retribution from their attackers, and/or being arrested themselves as runaways and returned to an abusive home environment or put in juvenile detention. Unfortunately this reality only compounds the situation while increasing the risk teenage prostitutes face for further victimization.

In an examination of the culture of violence homeless prostituted youth are immersed in, B. Schissel and K. Fedec found not only a high degree of child sexual and physical abuse experienced by the prostitute, but proposed that prostitution itself "creates a context in which those youth who are involved will run a high risk of being damaged by a predator or by themselves—whether directly through assault and self-injury or indirectly through high-risk behavior." Similarly, in another study of streetwalkers in Vancouver, Canada it was found that most had been physically and sexually abused prior to and after entering prostitution, and a very high percentage had been victims of dating violence.

Prostituted Youth and Child Pornography

Prostitution-involved youth and are often lured or forced into child pornography as another disturbing aspect of child sexual exploitation. Child pornography, also known as child porn or kiddie porn, is denned as "photographs, videos, books, magazines, and motion pictures that depict children in sexually explicit acts with other children, adults, animals, and/or foreign objects." Child pornography is a multibillion dollar international business that has moved onto the Internet and other digital devices as a means of further exploiting the innocent minors pornographers and pedophiles target. In the United States alone, child porn takes in as much as six billion dollars annually, exposing victims as young as five up to well into their late teens to "every form of child sexual exploitation, including molestation, rape, sadism, prostitution, bestiality, troilism, exhibitionism, voyeurism, and even murder."

Child pornographers often set their sights on runaway, thrownaway, and prostituted homeless youth because they are easily accessible, vulnerable to sexual exploitation, desperate enough to engage in survival sex and pornographic activities, and of fairly low risk for detection by law enforcement (though more aggressive efforts are being made these days to go after pornographers and purveyors of child porn and its customers), and often have mental health or substance abuse issues, further making these youth susceptible to victimization. Most victims of child pornography have been sexually abused at home and sexually victimized through prostitution, rape, sexual slavery, sex trafficking, and other sexual mistreatment as street kids. This puts them at even higher risk for sexually transmitted infections such as HIV. . . .

In many instances, pimps and pornographers are one and the same or work in conjunction in sexually exploiting children. According to the *Prostitution of Children and Child-Sex Tourism*, compelling prostituted female youth to participate in pornographic activities is another way for pimps to "control and humiliate the girl and break her resistance," as well as "normalize the practice of prostitution." In today's Internet age, some pimps use pornographic images of the girls in their stable to peddle them, while many clients and pedophiles photograph or videotape prostituted youth for their own perverse pleasures and collecting child porn.

The correlation between juvenile prostitution and child pornography often begins with the runaway or thrownaway turned street youth and homeless. As explained by teenage prostitution researcher Clare Tattersall: "You do not have to be a runaway to be forced into pornography. But because runaways are more likely to become prostitutes, they are also more likely to be forced into pornography." A survey of prostitution-involved teenagers found that about one in three were also involved in child pornography. The percentage of prostituted youth being exploited by pornographers is likely much higher.

In her study of prostituted youth in New York City, Mia Spangenberg reported that child prostitution is,

> . . . a continuum both in terms of the age of the young people involved and the range of exploitation. . . . Some youth work part-time, some full-time, and some are engaged in prostitution while others work in sex clubs, in the pornography business or both.

For many homeless teenagers looking for any means to survive living on the streets or feed a drug addiction, it may be hard to resist the lure of seemingly "easy" money that child pornographers often promise but can never deliver. While most prostituted youth become involved in pornography after entering the sex-for-sale business, others were initially recruited into child pornography before being coerced into prostitution, maximizing the potential for sexual exploitation.

Prostituted Youth and Police Contact

Though prostituted youth are generally regarded as victims of sexual and physical abuse and troubled histories and sexual exploitation, they are also subject to arrest as violators of prostitution laws that are in effect in every state where it concerns child prostitution. The delicate balance between victim and offender has made it difficult for law enforcement to handle cases of prostituted youth, who are mainly runaways, thrownaways, and/or homeless and often involved in prostitution as an act of desperation, drug addiction, or a lifestyle dictated by the street environment.

Arrests of prostitution-involved teenagers are often looked upon by police departments as a way to rescue or divert the victimized and sexually exploited youth from a difficult life. In many instances, however, police view prostituted youth in a manner consistent with adult prostituted individuals as sex offenders. Other times, the efforts and resources of law enforcement agencies are either inadequate or the reluctance of the prostituted youth too strong to keep them from returning to the streets or going back to an environment they ran from, which includes an abusive domicile or foster care. . . .

Recent years have seen a greater emphasis by law enforcement agencies on efforts to try and steer prostitution-involved youth away from the streets and/or pimps, as well as the juvenile justice system, while going after pimps, customers, pedophiles, pornographers, sex traffickers, and others who sexually exploit children. In addition to targeting traditional street prostitution, authorities are cracking down on the growing problem of teenage prostitution over the Internet, such as the popular Craigslist.

In an analysis of information taken from the FBI's National Incident-Based Reporting System (NIBRS), which gathers crime data known to law enforcement, for the years 1997 to 2000, David Finkelhor and Richard Ormrod profiled prostitution-involved juveniles. Among their findings were the following:

- The prostitution of juveniles had a greater likelihood of involving multiple offenders than prostituted adults police came across.

- Juvenile prostitution tended to take place more often outside and in large metropolitan areas.

- The likelihood was greater that police would treat prostitution-involved youth as offenders rather than victims of crime and sexual exploitation.

- Prostituted females and young prostitutes were more likely to be considered as victims than males and older prostitutes.

- Female juvenile prostitutes were more likely than prostituted male juveniles to be referred to social service agencies and elsewhere.

- Prostituted youth were less likely to be arrested than prostituted adults.

- More than six out of ten juvenile prostitution incidents involved male offenders.

- More than four in ten male juvenile prostitution incidents consisted of assisting/promoting prostitution.

- Almost nine in ten female juvenile prostitution incidents involved prostitution only.

- Around three in four juvenile prostitution incidents resulted in an arrest.

The researchers also found that among prostituted youth, virtually all the prostitution activities were segregated by gender. This is not too surprising, given that female and male juvenile prostitutes generally operate under different rules with different clientele within the same street subculture, with females typically having pimps who dictate their movement; whereas males tend to work independently, though they too can be controlled by others, such as older prostitutes, customers, pornographers, and drug dealers.

> *"Studies by the National Network for Youth show that 66% of males and 33% of females report being assaulted on the street and that significant numbers are victims of commercial sexual exploitation."*

Many Street Teens Become Physical or Sexual Victims

Maureen Blaha

Maureen Blaha is the executive director of the National Runaway Switchboard, a communication system for runaway and homeless youth.

A significant number of homeless street teens—66 percent of males and 33 percent of females—report being physically assaulted and victims of sexual exploitation. As stated in the following viewpoint, running away from home and being homeless leads such teens to a life fraught with peril. Whether the youth left home because of an abusive family environment, emotional problems, or dysfunction, he or she adopts a dangerous lifestyle.

Maureen Blaha, "On the Run to Nowhere," *USA Today* (magazine), January 1, 2009.
Reproduced by permission.

As you read, consider the following questions:

1. As stated in the article, how many young people between the ages of 12 and 17 run away every year?

2. How much more likely are runaway youth to become infected with HIV?

3. According to the viewpoint, how many homeless youth engage in survival sex? What is survival sex?

"The runaway and throwaway issue has been a silent crisis far too long. We badly need a little noise, and the hope is that government officials, educators, and ordinary citizens join in the clamor."

"Oh, we don't have a runaway problem here." Those were the words of a cab driver who was taking me to a bigcity airport. The exact location is irrelevant as I hear the comment all the time—and everywhere. The latest estimate is that 1,600,000–2,800,000 young people between the ages of 12 and 17 run away every year, yet the problem, it seems, is never "here." That in itself is a problem. With the essential help of volunteers, the National Runaway Switchboard (NRS) handles more than 100,000 calls annually from at-risk and runaway youth and their families, with the fastest growing group of callers being 12 years old and younger. Over the years, those calls have come from virtually every city and town in the nation. No place is immune, yet awareness, while growing, remains low. One of the reasons is image. The sullen-faced adolescent on the street may not be easy to love, and all too easy to write off as a "bad kid." Then too, parents of runaways often are hesitant to talk about it or even to report it. So, in the U.S. today, the pressing needs of runaway and at-risk youth fester as a silent crisis. The NRS's goal and that of its colleagues in the social service community is to change all that. . . .

Runaway Girls Are Victimized by Their Pimps

After using court records to compile a database of over a hundred convicted pimps and where each is incarcerated, *The New York Times* wrote letters to each more than two years ago. In the ensuing interviews by phone and in letters, more than two dozen convicted and still incarcerated pimps described the complicated roles they played as father figure, landlord, boss and boyfriend to the girls who worked for them. They said they went after girls with low self-esteem, prior sexual experience and a lack of options.

"With the young girls, you promise them heaven, they'll follow you to hell," said Harvey Washington, a pimp who began serving a four-year sentence in Arizona in 2005 for pandering a 17-year-old and three adult prostitutes. "It all depends on her being so love-drunk off of me that she will do anything for me."

Ian Urbina, "For Runaways, Sex Buys Survival," The New York Times, *October 27, 2009.*

Street life is fraught with peril. The Office of Juvenile Justice and Delinquency Prevention found that 71% of runaway and throwaway youth are "endangered," meaning they are more likely to have put themselves in dangerous situations, such as being substance dependent and hanging out in areas where criminal activity occurs. Studies by the National Network for Youth show that 66% of males and 33% of females report being assaulted on the street and that significant numbers are victims of commercial sexual exploitation. It follows that runaway youth are six to 12 times more likely to become infected with HIV than their at-home peers. On top of this is the developmental impact. Education falls by the wayside for most runaway and homeless youth. Shelter staff report that half of shelter youth 16 and older are out of school. Almost all are developmentally delayed. Teen pregnancy is prevalent. Nearly half the young women on the street and one-third of the girls in shelters report having been pregnant in the past.

What it comes down to is this: if that runaway or throw-away kid you see on the corner has a sullen look on his or her face, he or she probably earned it the hard way. Nobody wakes up in the morning and decides to adopt a dangerous lifestyle. The reasons for leaving home vary, but there always are reasons. Sometimes it is a dysfunctional, neglectful, or abusive family environment, or it could be the child's own emotional demons, changes in family structure—such as a divorce or re-marriage—or peer pressure that prompts the runaway episode.

In any event, the life out there is tough and its poisonous effects and economic impact touch us all. Runaway and throw-away young people sometimes turn to illegal and dangerous activities to survive. More than one-third of homeless youth engage in survival sex trading sex for money, food, shelter, drugs, and other subsistence needs. Almost as many report dealing drugs or engaging in other criminal activities to survive on the street. . . .

"*LGBTQ respondents reported experiencing an average of 7.4 more acts of sexual violence toward them than the heterosexual participants.*"

Gay and Transgender Street Youth Are at Greater Risk of Becoming Sexual Victims

James M. Van Leeuwen, Susan Boyle, Stacy Salomonsen-Sautel, D. Nico Baker, et al.

James M. Van Leeuwen is director of development and public affairs at Urban Peak, a service for homeless and runaway youth in Denver, Colorado. Susan Boyle is manager of outreach and substance abuse services at Urban Peak. Stacy Salomonsen-Sautel is a research assistant for the Department of Psychiatry at the University of Colorado at Denver. D. Nico Baker is housing case manager at Urban Peak.

There is a disproportionate number of gay and transgender youth on the street, and they face greater risks than their heterosexual peers, according to the following viewpoint. Studies reveal that homeless LGBTQ (lesbian, gay, bisexual, transgendered,

James M. Van Leeuwen, Susan Boyle, Stacy Salomonsen-Sautel, D. Nico Baker, et al., "Lesbian, Gay, and Bisexual Homeless Youth: An Eight-City Public Health Perspective," *Child Welfare*, March 1, 2006. Copyright © 2006 by Child Welfare League of America. All rights reserved. Reproduced by permission.

or questioning) youth are at greater risk for substance abuse, and being victims of both physical and sexual violence. Due to the stigma that is associated with an LGBTQ youth, there's a lack of support which exacerbates their vulnerability.

As you read, consider the following questions:

1. As stated in the article, the rates of sexual abuse of LGBTQ youth was how many more times higher than that of their heterosexual peers?

2. What is "survival sex"?

3. What percentage of LGB youth reported being asked to exchange sex for money?

This article reports on results of a one-day public health survey conducted in six states by homeless youth providers to measure and compare risk factors between lesbian, gay, and bisexual (LGB) homeless youth and non-LGB homeless youth. This article intends to inform the child welfare field on existing gaps in services and areas where more training and technical support is necessary in providing services to homeless LGB youth. The findings point to substantial differences within the homeless youth sample and demonstrate that in addition to the public health risks young people face merely by being homeless, the risks are exacerbated for those who self-identify as lesbian, gay, or bisexual. The article informs child welfare providers and policymakers about the substantial vulnerability of LGB youth beyond that of non-LGB homeless youth and the need to fund programming, training, technical assistance and further research to specifically respond to the complex needs of this population.

An estimated 1.6 million youth are homeless each year in the United States. Whitbeck, Chen, Hoyt, Tyler and Johnson estimate the average percentage of homeless youth who identify as lesbian, gay, bisexual, transgender, and questioning (LGBTQ) is approximately 20%, with a slightly smaller representation outside of large urban areas. In many cases, these youth are presenting agencies and service systems with very different needs and challenges that deserve attention in policy and program development. . . .

Homeless youth reported experiencing high levels of physical and sexual abuse, pervasive mental illness, and high rates of engaging in risky sexual behavior. A national study of 364 homeless adolescents found that 60% of girls and 23% of boys reported sexual abuse before leaving home, 51% reported being physically abused prior to leaving home, and 62% were afraid of being hit.

Rates of survival sex (the exchange of sex for drugs, money, food, clothing, or shelter) vary dramatically in the literature. Greene, Ennett, and Ringwalt report 28% of their street youth samples participated in survival sex, whereas Kipke, Unger, O'Connor, Palmer, and LaFrance estimate this behavior occurs in between 16% and 46% of street youth. Yates, MacKenzie, Pennbridge, and Cohen estimate that approximately 26% of the homeless and runaway youth in their sample were involved in survival sex. A survey of 206 runaways, ages 11–18 and living in New York City, revealed that among the 80% of sexually active youth, 22% of males and 7% of females engaged in survival sex. Rew concludes homeless youth were at high risk of contracting sexually transmitted infections because high-risk sexual behaviors were reported, including multiple sex partners and survival sex. . . .

These risk factors also are present among LGBTQ homeless youth and, in some cases, more pronounced. In general, LGBTQ youth are at greater risk for substance abuse and suicide, and they are at high risk for being both victims and perpetrators of physical violence compared to the general adolescent population. LGBTQ youth are affected further by stigma, lack of support, homophobia, engagement in sexual activity at a young age, contact with many sexual partners, and high rates of sexual coercion. LGBTQ adolescents report high rates of pregnancy, physical, and sexual abuse and experience obstacles to healthcare and mental health treatment. As a result of these public health factors, many youth become homeless, a situation that seems to exacerbate their vulnerability. . . .

Once homeless, this population is at higher risk for victimization than their heterosexual peers and present higher rates of psychopathology and unsafe sexual behavior. . . .

Cochran, Stewart, Ginzier, and Cauce find that LGBTQ respondents reported experiencing an average of 7.4 more acts of sexual violence toward them than the heterosexual participants. A recent study reports LGBTQ youth had higher rates of HIV infection and almost twice the rates of sexual victimization. Additionally, LGBTQ youth reported double the rates of sexual abuse before age 12. With respect to substance use, Noell and Ochs find that LGBTQ homeless youth are more likely to engage in amphetamine and injection drug use than non-LGBTQ homeless youth.

Methods

The authors report on results of a one-day public health survey conducted in six states by homeless youth providers in an effort to measure and compare risk factors between lesbian, gay, and bisexual (LGB) and non-LGB homeless youth. Because of the small sample size of transgender youth (n = 7), the authors decided not to combine transgender with LGB and do not have any information on questioning youth. To the authors' knowledge, only one other study compares LGB and non-LGB among homeless youth. This article is important because it adds to the literature and builds on a very limited body of research about this population by analyzing a series of public health risk factors that previously have not been investigated. The literature indicates that independently being homeless or identifying as LGBTQ increases public health risks for young people.

This article examines the public health risks of being both homeless and LGB. The findings have important effects for both policymakers and providers in how they respond to the complex needs of this underresearched and marginalized population of youth. The value of this study is underscored by an assessment of Slesnick describing homeless and runaway youth as an "understudied and ignored population, primarily due to methodological challenges in locating, treating, and retaining youth in treatment." . . .

Risk Factors

In comparison to non-LGB youth, LGB youth reported significantly more risk factors. More LGB youth (44%) than non-LGB youth (32%) reported ever being in the custody of social services. A significant difference appeared in suicide attempts. Sixty-two percent of LGB youth ever attempted suicide in contrast to 29% of non-LGB youth.

A significant difference also appeared between LGB youth and non-LGB youth in survival sex. More LGB youth (44%) than non-LGB youth (26%) reported ever being asked by someone on the streets to exchange sex for money, food, drugs, shelter, clothing, and more. This significant difference also occurred for actually trading sex for material supplies (19% of LGB vs. 8% of non-LGB).

> "Living in non-family settings, with its associated lack of supervision and lack of social support, increases newly homeless youth's sexual risk-taking behaviors."

Many Street Teens Indulge in Risky Sexual Behavior

M. Rosa Solorio, Doreen Rosenthal, Norweeta G. Milburn, Robert E. Weiss, Philip J. Batterham, Marla Gandara, and Mary Jane Rotheram-Borus

Homeless youth are more likely to engage in unsafe sexual behaviors that put them at risk for sexually transmitted diseases including AIDS, claim the authors of the following viewpoint. They cite research to support their hypothesis that adolescents living without family supervision and adolescents who are substance abusers tend to have more sexual partners and are less likely to use condoms than other homeless teens. M. Rosa Solorio is on the faculty of the School of Public Health and Community Medicine at the University of Washington. Doreen Rosenthal is professor of women's health at the University of Melbourne, where she is also director of the Key Centre for Women's Health

M. Rosa Solorio, Doreen Rosenthal, Norweeta G. Milburn, Robert E. Weiss, Philip J. Batterham, Marla Gandara, and Mary Jane Rotheram-Borus, "Predictors of Sexual Risk Behaviors Among Newly Homeless Youth: A Longitudinal Study," *Journal of Adolescent Health*, vol. 42, no. 4, April 2008, pp. 401–09. Copyright © 2008 by Elsevier. All rights reserved. Reproduced by permission.

in Society. Norweeta G. Milburn and Philip J. Batterham are researchers at the Jane and Terry Semel Institute for Neuroscience and Human Behavior at the University of California-Los Angeles (UCLA). Mary Jane Rotheram-Borus is a professor of clinical psychology and principal investigator of the Center for HIV Identification, Prevention, and Treatment Services at UCLA. Robert E. Weiss is a professor in the department of biostatistics in the School of Public Health at UCLA. Marla Gandara is a resident in emergency medicine at the University of California, San Francisco, Fresno Medical Education and Research.

As you read, consider the following questions:

1. What characteristics do the authors suggest may make teens more susceptible to engaging in risky sexual behaviors?

2. What gender differences did the authors find in sexual risk behaviors?

3. What recommendations do the authors have for reducing sexual risk behaviors?

A dolescent homelessness is a national concern. According to a survey, based on a representative national sample, 7.6% of adolescents have been homeless at some time in [1997]. Homeless youth are known to engage in risky sexual behaviors that increase their risk for sexually transmitted diseases (STDs) and human immunodeficiency virus (HIV). Some homeless youth may be at additional risk due to their history of childhood sexual abuse, early sexual debut, depression, alcohol and drug abuse, living on the street, as well as a lack of connectedness to trusted adults and family. In addition, previous studies report that sexual risk behaviors vary by gender and by sexual orientation. Homeless adolescent females compared to males, engage in more sex acts, are more likely to trade sex for money, food, drugs, or shelter, and are less likely to use condoms. Homeless young males who have sex with other males report having more sexual partners than males who have sex with females only. Most studies to date on homeless youth sexual risk behaviors have been cross-sectional and not longitudinal studies[1]. While the previous studies mentioned have examined the association between homeless youth individual factors and their association with sexual risk, few studies have examined the association between structural factors (living situation) and sexual risk behaviors.

Therefore, the goal of this study is to longitudinally examine the association between newly homeless youth (NHY) individual factors (sociodemographic characteristics, depression, substance use) and structural factors (living situation) with sexual risk behaviors.

Substance Abusers and Teens Without Family Structure Are at Risk

NHY are distinguished from chronically homeless youth by the duration of time that they have spent away from home. NHY have been away from home for more than one day but less than six months. Knowledge about the characteristics of NHY has recently increased and it [is] now known that the characteristics of these youth vary from those who are chronically homeless. NHY tend to return home by 12 months (65%), they typically leave home due to family conflict (not sexual abuse), and only 1.4% report trading sex for money, food, drugs, or shelter. Since a large percentage of newly homeless youth may return home by 12 months and since the living situation may change over time, with some youth remaining at home and others running away from home again, at a future time, a longitudinal evaluation of newly homeless youth may allow for an examination of the effect of living situation on sexual risk behaviors. . . .

Social Cognitive Theory suggests that complex behaviors (i.e, engaging in positive health practices to avoid disease) are

1. Longitudinal studies analyze the same set of behaviors over a long period of time.

associated with perceived self-efficacy (the belief that one can perform the desired behavior) and outcome expectancies (the belief that engaging in a particular behavior leads to the desired outcome). According to this theory, positive sexual health practices such as consistent use of condoms and sexual self-care behaviors, such as avoiding casual sex with multiple partners, represent one endpoint of a complex process that involves cognitive-perceptual factors (i.e. sexual knowledge, future time perspective, perceived health status, self-efficacy for using condoms, intentions to use condoms, perceived social support) and behavioral factors in assertive communication and help-seeking to avoid or manage STD symptoms. Based on Social Cognitive Theory and previous studies on homeless youth sexual risk behaviors, for this study, two hypothesis will be evaluated: 1) youth living in housing situations without parental supervision and support will report more sexual partners and less condom use (for this study social support is implied by youth living with family members; actual social support was not measured); 2) youth who are substance abusers will report more sexual partners and less condom use. . . .

The Theory Was Confirmed by the Results

Our homeless youth sample included 29.9% African Americans, 33% U.S.-born Latinos, 14.6% foreign-born Latinos, 22.6% Caucasian/Asian/Pacific Islander/American Indian/Alaskan Native youth and 59.8% were female (only 1.0% self-identified as lesbian/bisexual), 33.0% of males self-identified as heterosexual and 7.3% as gay/bisexual. The mean age was 15.5 years. At the baseline assessment, 78.2% were living in an institution such as a shelter, 10% with family, and 11.9% in non-family arrangements. Sixteen percent of the youth met BSI [Brief Symptom Inventory, a psychological assessment] criteria for depression or anxiety. A previous study on this cohort of youth indicates that the main reason for leaving home is family conflict and that by 12 months of follow-up, 65% of youth were living back at home.

At baseline, 77% of youth had been sexually active, increasing to 85% of youth at 24 months of follow-up. Reports of sexual activity in the past 3 months varied among the youth at the baseline assessment: 51.3% of youth had not been sexually active, 30.7% had one serious sexual partner, 5.0% had multiple serious partners, 7.3% had serious and casual partners, and 5.8% had multiple casual partners. For condom use at baseline, among those having sex, 22% never used condoms, 43% sometimes used condoms, and 35% always used condoms. The mean number of sexual partners was 1.5 at baseline.

Teens in a Non-Family Setting Have More Sexual Partners

In evaluating the association between living situation and multiple sexual partners, for male youth, those living in a non-family setting were found to be more likely to report more sexual partners than those living with family or in institution, thus, supporting our hypothesis; however, for females there was no significant association between living situation and number of sexual partners. Among females, the factors associated with having multiple sexual partners included time in study, age, drug use, and race/ethnicity, with Caucasian/Asian/Pacific Islander/American Indian/Alaskan Native females being more likely to have multiple partners than Latinas (U.S.-born or foreign-born).

To assess condom use, we selected youth who had been sexually active and removed those who had never had sex in the 24 months of follow-up, for a sample size of 207. At baseline 77% of youth had been sexually active, but by 24 months of follow-up this percentage had increased to 85%. The association between living situation and condom use was assessed. For females, living in a non-family setting was associated with decreased odds of always using condoms compared to those living with family or in an institution, this finding supported our hypothesis. In addition, for females, drug use, regardless of type of sexual partner (whether monogamous vs. casual partner), was associated with decreased odds of always using condoms. For males, no covariates were found to be associated with condom use.

Substance Abusers Have More Sexual Partners

For both males and females, drug use was significantly and positively associated with having more sexual partners, these findings support our hypothesis. For females, using drugs (regardless of partner type) decreased the odds of always using condoms; this finding supported our hypothesis. For males, however, drug use was not associated with condom use.

The study findings on the association between living situation and having multiple sexual partners and condom use, confirmed our hypotheses, in part. Living in a non-family setting, compared to living with family or in an institutional setting, was found to be associated with having multiple sexual partners, among males only. Also, living in a non-family setting was found to decrease the odds of always using condoms, among females only. These findings illustrate the importance of addressing structural factors, such as housing, when aiming to reduce homeless youth's sexual risk behaviors (multiple sexual partners or condom use). It is likely that youth who live with family or in institutional settings receive more supervision and more social support than those living with non-family settings and that these factors in turn influence youth's sexual risk behaviors. These findings are consistent with Social Cognitive Theory; social support may influence sexual health practices.

A strong association between alcohol and drug use (marijuana, hard drugs, injecting drugs) and having multiple sexual partners for both males and females was found. This finding is consistent with a previous study on homeless adolescents which found an association between drug use and number of sexual partners and with a study on domiciled adolescents that found that marijuana use and binge drinking were associated with having multiple sexual partners in young adulthood. In our study, Latina females (whether U.S.-born or foreign-born) were less likely to have multiple sexual partners than Caucasian/Asian/Pacific Islander/American Indian/ Alaskan Native females. This finding is consistent with previous research on domiciled Latina and Caucasian female adolescents in California.

For condom use among females, living in a non-family setting and using drugs decreased the odds of always using condoms; for drug use, this was true regardless of whether type of sexual partner was serious or casual. These findings illustrate that when drug use is taken into account, youth who use drugs are less likely to use condoms, regardless of type of partner (serious vs. casual). These findings differ from previous studies. One previous study on homeless youth found that having one sexual partner was associated with the nonuse of condoms; however drug use was not taken into account. A previous study on domiciled youth reports that the greatest risk for not using condoms is being in a stable relationship with one partner. . . .

The longitudinal evaluation of this cohort of newly homeless youth shows that living in non-family settings, with its associated lack of supervision and lack of social support, increases newly homeless youth's sexual risk-taking behaviors. While gender and some racial/ethnic differences in predictors of sexual risk were found in this study, living with non-family members and drug use appear to be the most salient in explaining sexual risk. Our findings indicate that interventions aimed at reducing sexual risk behaviors, and thereby reducing STDs and HIV among newly homeless youth, need to help youth find housing associated with supervision and social support (family and institutional settings) as well as aim to reduce drug use.

Periodical and Internet Sources Bibliography

The following articles have been selected to supplement the diverse views presented in this chapter.

HealthHype.com	"Newly Homeless Youth Are at High Risk with Sexual Behavior," January 11, 2008. www.healthhype.com.
Sean A. Kidd and Larry Davidson	"You Have to Adapt Because You Have No Other Choice: The Stories of Strength and Resilience—208 Homeless Youth in New York City and Toronto," *Journal of Community Psychology*, vol. 35, no. 2, 2007, pp. 219–38.
Pat LaMarche	"Homeless Teens More Often Denied Shelter and Separated from Families," *Huffington Post*, January 29, 2011. Huffingtonpost.com.
Joe Piasecki	"Throwaway Kids," *Pasadena Weekly*, June 22, 2006. www.pasadenaweekly.com.
S. Ramashwar	"Feelings of Abandonment May Predict Pregnancy Among Homeless Adolescents," *Perspectives on Sexual and Reproductive Health*, vol. 40, no. 4, December 2008, pp. 242–43.
Sanna J. Thompson et al.	"Runaway and Pregnant: Risk Factors Associated with Pregnancy in a National Sample of Runaway/Homeless Female Adolescents," *Journal of Adolescent Health*, vol. 43, no. 2, 2008, pp. 125 32.
Ian Urbina	"For Runaways, Sex Buys Survival," *New York Times*, October 27, 2009. www.nytimes.com.
Chelsea Warren and Erica Teichert	"Runaways Have Tough Life on Street," *Universe*, May 31, 2009. Newsnet.byu.edu.

OPPOSING
VIEWPOINTS®
SERIES

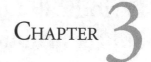
CHAPTER 3

How Can Street Teens Be Helped?

Chapter Preface

Shelley is a youth shelter success story. She was dropped off at the Bill Wilson Center's youth shelter in Santa Clara, California, by her mother, reports the executive director and CEO of the center, Sparky Harlan in a web posting titled "What Keeps Me Awake at Nights . . .". A physical examination revealed burn marks, where Shelley's mother had punished her by burning her with cigarettes. Another form of punishment her mother inflicted was keeping Shelley home from school, so the abused seventeen-year-old was on the verge of failing her senior year. By working with social workers and administrators from Shelley's school, the shelter was able to get her counseling, help her with her appearance, take her shopping, help her with social skills, and, most importantly, find her a supportive foster home and ensure she graduated with her class.

In an article on the website Black Angels, Peter Whoriskey relates a story without a happy ending in "How System Failed Cynteria." Cynteria was taken from her drug addict mother and abusive father when she was six years old and placed in the first of eight foster homes she would live in over the next seven years. During the last seven months of her life, she ran away from her last foster home, lived on the streets of Miami, Florida, and occasionally dropped in on relatives she barely knew. Twice during this time, relatives called the police and asked that Cynteria be placed in a shelter. Before she ran away for the last time, she was staying at Miami Bridge, which is not a locked facility and cannot keep teens from running away. Judge Steven Robinson, who handled Cynteria's case, said, "Had Cynteria been placed in a shelter with security, she could have been psychologically evaluated and offered professional counseling." Instead, she was found nude, sexually molested, beaten, and dead on the streets of Miami—a case that took ten years to solve.

While there are varying opinions on the effectiveness of the youth shelter and foster care systems, virtually all experts agree that street teens are better off in well-run youth shelters or foster homes than on the street. On any given day, at least two hundred thousand children in the United States are homeless. In most cases, there was a stressful event or series of events that caused the child to leave home. Being homeless introduces additional stressors. According to the National Child Traumatic Stress Network (NCTSN), homeless children experience a loss of community, routines, possessions, privacy, and security, and are more vulnerable to sexual and physical assault. In addition, homeless children are sick at twice the rate of other children, go hungry twice as often, and have twice the rate of learning disabilities and three times the rate of emotional and behavioral problems. Approximately one-half of school-age homeless children suffer anxiety, depression, or withdrawal compared to 18 percent of other children, according to the NCTSN.

Street children without a support network of friends or relatives can find refuge and support in community-based shelters. Well-run shelters can help street teens by minimizing the risks they are exposed to, connecting them to health services and counseling, and helping them to find a more permanent home. Shelters, foster care, and other means of helping street teens are debated in the viewpoints in the following chapter.

| "The number of beds at either one of the Chicago hostels is more than for all of Britain's youth refuges put together."

The UK Should Emulate the US Model for Sheltering Street Teens

Kira Cochrane

The scarcity of shelters for runaway children in the UK is shocking, with ten beds available to support an annual runaway total of 100,000, according to Kira Cochrane in the following viewpoint. The United States does a far better job of providing shelter for its runaways, with the federal government providing funding for a large network of resources, including 345 basic shelters. The Children's Society of the UK is running a Safe and Sound campaign, calling for a refuge in each of Britain's ten regions, the author reports. Kira Cochrane is a features writer for the Guardian.

As you read, consider the following questions:

1. What does the author cite as some of the cultural changes that are making conditions more difficult for street children?

Kira Cochrane, "Our Young Runaways," *New Statesman*, April 3, 2006. Copyright © 2006 by New Statesman. All rights reserved. Reproduced by permission.

2. Why are some children reluctant to use social services, according to the author?

3. What percentage of runaways leave home more than once, according to the author?

The girl hunched beside me on the couch is wearing a huge black poncho that covers everything except the nervous tap of her feet. Leila, a pale girl in her late teens, is seventh in a family of 17 kids. She is bipolar, and her mother was a drug addict who committed suicide just before Thanksgiving last year [2005]. Her natural father is blind and wants nothing to do with her; her stepfather abused her. "I said to my mum, it's him or me, and she just told me to get out." By the age of 14 Leila was homeless, by 15 she had a son, and by 16 she was regularly taking crystal meth, cocaine, crack and angel dust. "I did drugs even before I was on the streets, though," she notes. "I started doing them with my mum."

The US Has a Large Network of Shelters

Despite all this Leila is feeling pretty good. She recently completed eight months of rehab. "I feel fine today. Being homeless obviously isn't great, but when you have somewhere like this to go"—she gestures around the large, bright common room we are sitting in, and shrugs—"well, it's much better than sleeping on a park bench, isn't it?"

Leila is staying at the Open Door Youth Shelter, a 16-bed emergency refuge for 14- to 21-year-olds in Chicago's Lakeview neighbourhood. Run by a charity called the Night Ministry, it offers refuge day and night (unlike adult shelters, which tend to open only from 9PM to 7AM). It is one of 345 basic centres across the United States which draw their core funding from the federal government and form part of a huge national network of resources to which runaway children can be referred.

I'm in Chicago on a fact-finding visit organised by a British charity, the Children's Society. With me are the Liberal Democrat MP [Ministers of Parliament] Paul Burstow and members of the Metropolitan Police. The Night Ministry is about to open another, 24-bed, shelter in Chicago, which will offer much-needed additional refuge to the estimated 25,000 of the city's children who run away from home overnight each year. The number of beds it provides—a total of 40 in the two shelters—might not sound like a lot, but it is generous compared to British provision.

The UK Has Few Shelters

Indeed, the number of beds at either one of the Chicago hostels is more than for all of Britain's youth refuges put together. A six-bed refuge in London, a three-bed refuge in Scotland and a one-bed refuge in Devon together provide just ten emergency beds for Britain's entire young runaway population. This is shocking, given that each year in the UK 100,000 children under the age of 16 flee their homes. A quarter of these are under 11; some are as young as six.

The most common reason for running away is family conflict or physical abuse. One in six runaway children sleeps rough or in the homes of strangers, significantly increasing the potential for harm. "When people think of street children," says Emilie Smeaton, a senior researcher at the Children's Society, "they tend to think of Africa or Brazil. Since I started doing research into this area in the late 1990s, though, conditions have become much worse for our own street children, with gang culture increasing rapidly and drug use changing, too—the prices have gone right down. We're seeing runaway children getting involved with dangerous behaviours much earlier: having sex and taking drugs at age ten or 11, for instance."

In response, the Children's Society is running a Safe and Sound campaign, calling on the government to fund an integrated national network of resources for runaways, including independently run children's refuges. It has been mooted that there should be one for each of Britain's ten regions.

Burstow's early-day motion on the matter, tabled last year, has been backed by 340 MPs. "I think the most striking thing for me has been that this one youth shelter here in Chicago has more beds than we have in the whole of the UK," he says. "The runaway issue is out of sight, out of mind for us right now, the problem being that there's no part of the country where there's a critical mass of runaway children. Without that, it's possible to ignore the issue. The closest we have to a critical mass is in London, and there the shelter exists hand to mouth. That's why, in this case, some kind of national statutory framework is necessary."

Runaways Don't Get Top Priority

Some would argue that existing social services and local council provision should be adequate to deal with the problem. With limited finances, however, social services are frequently forced to prioritise cases, and teenage runaways understandably rank lower than, say, a five-year-old being removed from abusive parents.

A case in point is 18-year-old Carl Hillier, a former runaway from Weymouth, who has joined us on the trip to Chicago. In January last year a long-standing series of arguments between Carl and his mother escalated into a crisis. "It was a Sunday night and the arguments had been going on for about five hours," he recalls, "until she just said, 'I think the best thing is that you leave.' In that moment I thought, 'Yeah, I actually have to go,' so I grabbed my jumper and left.

"For the first few minutes I thought, 'Thank God,' but the next feeling was, 'Oh shit, it's 12.30am and I've got nowhere to go.' I'd been a peer mediator at school, so I had a number for the Runaway Helpline [part of the National Missing Per-

A Covenant House Success Story

Jodie came to Covenant House having survived horrific physical abuse from her mother. She wouldn't talk about it, but we knew that the emotional scars were there. What we didn't know, however, was that inside this vulnerable girl was another dark secret.

"Here," Jodie said, thrusting the phone at her Crisis Care counselor at Covenant House, "It's my friend. He's gonna give you the address so you can write it down."

We quickly realized that Jodie wasn't asking for a favor... she was asking us to write it down because she couldn't read or write at all.

Betrayed by her mother in so many ways, Jodie struggled to survive—often in a world she wasn't able to fully understand—but Covenant House is helping her learn, understand, and find her way.

"Overcoming Homelessness Through Healthcare,"
Covenant House. www.covenanthouse.org.

sons Helpline] and I rang that. They put me through to social services in Poole, 50 miles away, who said that because it was the middle of the night, there was nothing they could do. They had absolutely nowhere for me to go."

In the US, the federal government provides core funding for the National Runaway Switchboard, a well-publicised and centralised toll-free service that offers help to runaways or parents and friends of runaways, and which can refer them to the most local and appropriate of the country's 17,000 resources. The Runaway Helpline is the British equivalent. It does a great job, fielding 8,000 calls a month on average, but it is hampered by a lack of on-the-ground provision. Vanessa

Gray, who heads the service, has said that the facilities for vulnerable children are often "patchy, inaccessible, and in some instances non-existent".

Some Children Are Afraid to Approach Social Services

Even if social services had the money to provide adequate resources, it is doubtful that a lot of young runaways would approach them. "We know that many children are afraid to run to social services because of what they've heard about being in the care system," says Martin Houghton-Brown, policy adviser at the Children's Society. "They're frightened of the situation that they're running from, and we don't want to create a situation where they're afraid of running to a resource."

The proposed refuges, run by independent organisations but with core funding from the government, would offer a confidential breathing space for up to ten days. In this setting, runaway children could access advice about what to do next. Ideally, a long-term solution would be found; foster care, for instance, or returning home with the help of family mediation. It is estimated that these refuges would cost about £1m a year each, but they would seem to make good financial sense. Lancashire Police has estimated that it costs roughly £1,200 to investigate one runaway incident, and in most cases the child is returned home without a resolution. Unsurprisingly, this often leads to children bolting again—57 per cent of runaways leave home more than once, and some leave up to a hundred times in a year.

There is also evidence that such breathing space might cut other housing costs. For instance, Carl ended up living in a local youth project for nine months before returning home. "Me and my mum are actually closer than ever now," he says, "but it took all that time for the situation to improve. I think that if a refuge had been available for a couple of weeks, combined with some family mediation, it's more than likely I would have gone straight home when it was time to leave the refuge."

In Chicago, the future for Leila looks more positive than it has in years. Her son is living with his father and paternal grandmother in California, and they have made a deal that she can join them when she's been clean for a year. Just four months to go. There's also the possibility of a job at the rehab centre she attended, if she can stay clean for two years.

"I grew up in a large family, so I'm used to this kind of environment," she says, nodding at her surroundings. "I like it. I'm safe, I get fed, I get clothed. There's nothing to worry about." Her smile is wan, but genuine. "I honestly don't think I could feel better than I do right now."

> "While the number of shelters and other institutions that help runaways [has] slowly increased over the decades, they have been unable to keep pace with the demand."

US Shelters Are Inadequate for the Needs of Street Teens

Martha Irvine

Although organizations like the National Runaway Switchboard do a good job of serving homeless teens, they are unable to keep up with the increasing demand for resources, according to Martha Irvine in the following viewpoint. Additionally, runaway adolescents are dealing with more complex issues today, with more of them trying to cope with substance or physical abuse or mental health issues. Tough economic conditions mean that funding for shelters has remained flat; at the same time, these conditions have greatly increased the need for shelters, the author argues. Martha Irvine is a national writer for the Associated Press.

As you read, consider the following questions:

1. What growth in the number of callers from 2000 to 2007 did the National Runaway Switchboard report, according to Irvine?

2. What percentage growth in the number of callers from 2000 to 2007 claiming abuse did the National Runaway Switchboard report, according to Irvine?

3. What growth in the number of callers under the age of 13 from 2000 to 2007 did the National Runaway Switchboard report, according to the author?

The young caller's voice is high-pitched and trembling.

Her mother's been drinking, she says. They got into a fistfight, so the girl grabbed her backpack and a cell phone and bolted, with little thought about where a 13-year-old could go on a cold night.

Hiding in an alley off her rural hometown's deserted main street, she calls the only phone number she can think of: 1-800-RUNAWAY.

"I just don't feel like I'm taken care of like a daughter should be," the girl tells the volunteer who answers the phone at the National Runaway Switchboard. She stutters between sobs and shivers.

Her story is a common one at the Chicago-based hot line, which handles well over 100,000 calls each year, many from troubled young people who are dealing with increasingly difficult issues.

National Runaway Switchboard data provided exclusively to The Associated Press shows that the overall number of young callers facing crises that jeopardized their safety rose from 13,650 in 2000 to 15,857 last year. About two-thirds of the latter figure were young people who were thinking of running away, had already done so or had been thrown out of the house.

Federally funded since the 1970s, the National Runaway Switchboard is regarded by people who work with troubled youth as an organization that provides one of the best overviews of the shadowy world of teenage runaways, which is difficult to track.

The group's statistics showed that callers are getting younger and that 6,884 crisis callers last year said they had been abused or neglected, compared with 3,860 in 2000. That is a 78 percent increase.

Some callers just want someone to talk to, about problems at home or with friends. Others who have already run away use the hot line to exchange messages with their families, to let them know they're OK, or to arrange a free bus ticket home.

Some are desperate for a place to stay, for safety, for options.

"I'm scared of my parents, and I don't want to go back there. Please don't make me!" pleaded the 13-year-old girl who called this particular night.

The information she gave the hot line checked out. However, her name and other identifying details could not be included for this story because the National Runaway Switchboard guarantees callers confidentiality.

It also quickly became apparent to volunteer Megan McCormick, who has been trained to spot the occasional crank call, that this girl's fear was real.

"I know it must be really scary," said McCormick, a graduate student in social work at the University of Chicago. As they spoke, she checked the call center's extensive computer database for shelters in the girl's hometown.

The closest was in a larger city, 40 minutes away. But when McCormick called, she was told they didn't take anyone younger than 14.

Such scenarios are common in many regions of the country, particularly rural areas where resources for runaways are scarce. Further complicating the matter, the Runaway Switchboard has found that more crisis callers than ever are 14 and younger—1,255 in that age group in 2000, compared with 1,844 last year.

"The reality is, there are not always services available for kids who are calling," says Maureen Blaha, executive director of the National Runaway Switchboard, which began as a Chicago area crisis hot line in 1971 and went national three years later. "We try to be as creative as we can be to find solutions. But there isn't always a simple answer."

Others in the youth services field concur.

They note that while the number of shelters and other organizations that help runaways [has] slowly increased over the decades, they have been unable to keep pace with the demand. Many institutions also lack the resources to deal with the severity of issues young people face today.

"The population is much more disturbed than the runaways who were being seen 20 or 30 years ago," says Victoria Wagner, chief executive of the National Network for Youth, a coalition of agencies that serve troubled young people. "There are more mental health issues, more substance abuse, more coming from violent home situations."

Long-standing government support for the Runaway Switchboard has been a vital component in addressing the problem, Wagner says. But, she adds, federal dollars for shelters and other services, also through the Runaway Youth Act, have remained largely stagnant since it first passed in the 1970s. So she and others are pressing Congress for more.

It's a tough sell in trying economic times. But the irony, Wagner says, is that when people are unemployed and families are struggling, young people are even more likely to have reason to run.

The 13-year-old girl who has called the Runaway Switchboard sounds even more anguished when McCormick tells there are no shelters in her area that will take her.

"So there's nowhere I can go?" she says in disbelief.

Several times McCormick asks about other options, but the girl says she has none.

She says her friends' parents would only take her back home. Relatives, whom she rarely sees, live out of state. And she seems even more afraid of her father than her mom, claiming that her parents divorced because he was abusive.

Even so, she has little doubt that one or both of her parents will soon be out looking for her.

That's not the case for many other runaways, who are thrown out of home for anything from being gay to exhibiting aggressive behavior.

"Ninety-eight percent of the time, it's the parents saying, 'No, take them.' They're the throwaway kids," says Bill Hogan, program manager at the Haven W. Poe Runaway Shelter in Tampa, Fla. He recently reunited a 10-year-old boy with his grandmother, who had told police to keep him.

Neglect also has changed the face of the runaway, says Kathleen Boutin, executive director of the Nevada Partnership for Homeless Youth, which is getting more requests for help from children of methamphetamine addicts.

For those 12 to 18, Nevada now has a "Right to Shelter" law, which allows organizations to provide emergency housing, food and clothing without parental consent.

Indiana is another state that recently passed a comprehensive law for homeless youth with a similar provision, but limited the age to 16 and older.

"It's a beginning," says Cynthia Smith, executive director of the Youth Service Bureau in Evansville, Ind. Right now, her area has no youth shelter, but she hopes the new law will help change that.

In New York, however, a bill requiring safe-houses and other services for sexually exploited youth stalled in January. And in Wyoming, runaways often still spend the night in jail.

It's a mind-set that Rusty Booker, an 18-year-old former runaway from Louisville, Ky., hopes will change.

Last year, he told members of Congress how, at age 12, he ran away from an abusive home. He got help at a library affiliated with National Safe Place, an organization with more than 16,000 locations nationally where young people are put in touch with local crisis workers.

Still, many communities that want to establish Safe Places are turned down because they have few or no services to offer runaways.

Nine states have no Safe Places at all. That includes the home of the 13-year-old girl who was on the line with the Runaway Switchboard for more than an hour.

Several times, she adamantly refused to call the local sheriff or to get child protective services involved.

"All this stuff that's going on, it's just really overwhelming," she told McCormick, the call center volunteer. "I don't want my mom to go to jail. I can't do that to my family."

Eventually, though, she changed her mind. She asked McCormick to stay on the line while she spoke with a county social worker and then the sheriff.

"I've kind of run away from home," the girl told the sheriff's dispatch operator. "I need somewhere to stay." McCormick waited on the line until a sheriff's deputy found her and picked her up. Finally, the girl was safe and members of the Runaway Switchboard staff looked relieved.

"You get used to some aspects of this," says Cori Ballew, a Runaway Switchboard supervisor who oversaw the call. "But you never get used to some of it, especially when it ends with no resolution."

Some runaways, like this one, find help of some kind, she says.

Others, faced with few choices, hang up.

> *"Only when someone is in a safe, reliable place can they begin to work on other life issues."*

Street Teens Are Better Off in Foster or Group Homes

Meghan Stromberg

Today's efforts to combat homelessness among teens center around finding appropriate and safe housing, according to Meghan Stromberg in the following viewpoint. The best solution for younger runaways is a foster or group home; the best solution for older runaways is a transitional living program. Existing programs not only provide shelter but also training in basic life skills and educational and job opportunities. Meghan Stromberg is a senior editor at Planning *magazine.*

As you read, consider the following questions:

1. What are some of the dangers homeless teens face, according to the author?

2. What are some of the many reasons kids become homeless, according to the author?

3. What social issue does the author find to be at the root of teen homelessness?

Meghan Stromberg, "Shadow Kids," *Planning*, vol. 72, no. 6, June 2006. Copyright © 2006 by American Planning Association. All rights reserved. Reproduced by permission.

According to Tim King's last count, taken at 3 a.m. on March 31 this year [2006], 125 young people were sleeping outside in Daley Plaza. They had built shelters from the rain using what they had on hand, mostly sections of wooden pallets and pieces of cardboard. Some were lucky enough to have sleeping bags. And fortunately for all of them, it was a warmer than usual spring night in Chicago—the temperature was in the 40s.

Earlier that day, King—cochair of the Youth Homelessness Team of the local youth advocacy group, Public Action for Change Today [PACT]—and five other representatives had requested a meeting with Mayor Richard M. Daley to discuss their concerns about homeless youth. Nearly 200 supporters rallied outside in the plaza named for the current leader's father, longtime Chicago mayor Richard J. Daley. When the meeting was denied—for the fourth time since December, King notes—the young people set up camp and slept outside in protest.

Among other things, the group sought was full funding of the mayor's 10-Year Plan to End Homelessness, a pilot program to make transit passes available to homeless young people, passage of a set-aside ordinance for new housing, and funding directed specifically at homeless youth programs.

The young people in Chicago expressed a common frustration felt by homeless teens (and the people who look out for them): Homeless young people are different from the adult homeless population and they tend to get overlooked.

"Homeless people in general, and kids in particular, really do slip through the cracks," says Melissa Maguire, director of the Youth Shelter Network of the nonprofit, nondenominational Chicago organization, The Night Ministry, which serves homeless and low-income youth and adults in a variety of ways. "And, they've got those same developmental issues as [teens] who aren't homeless, but for them there's no safety net [of parental support]," she adds.

A Boy Named Aaron

For some of the young people camping in Daley Plaza this past March, sleeping out in public or in an unsafe place was a familiar experience. King's cochair at PACT, Aaron Bowen, became homeless in the fall of 2004 at age 19. Now 21, Bowen is employed and plans to attend the University of Chicago in the fall. He currently lives in a single-room-occupancy [SRO] apartment, provided through the nonprofit Heartland Alliance for Human Needs and Human Rights.

The short version of the story goes like this: Bowen moved in with his mother after returning from college, but they couldn't overcome "issues of his lifestyle," he says. Bowen, who refers to himself as queer identified, was physically abused and finally kicked out of the house.

He, like many homeless teens, "couch-surfed," staying for a few nights or weeks with a friend or relative, but maintaining friendships was hard and eventually impossible. "My friends couldn't take care of me," Bowen says. They also couldn't relate to him or his situation.

People on the streets weren't any more helpful. Bowen stayed with acquaintances, many of whom would toss him out when he didn't pay his way—with sex—after a few days. One employer let him stay for a week or two before sexually assaulting him and robbing him of his savings account and all his personal possessions.

He became resourceful—sleeping on trains, showering at the gym, and walking dogs to make money. But the good-looking young man says he got little sympathy from other street people, and was told again and again, "Why don't you just go be an escort?"

"I've studied abroad, got into Yale," Bowen says. He never figured he'd have to trade his body for food or shelter. "I was taken advantage of by a lot of people," he says. "It was very, very painful."

Teenage Wasteland

Bowen's story is not unique. Homeless teens, properly referred to as unaccompanied homeless youth, are an extremely vulnerable group. More than half of them report being "beaten up" while on the streets, according to the National Alliance to End Homelessness, and the rates of sexual assault of homeless youth range from 15 to 20 percent. Homeless youth and youth service providers report that adult homeless shelters are among the most dangerous places to be.

Contrary to popular belief, homeless youth workers say, kids who run away and become homeless aren't bad kids who just want to rebel. "There's a perception that homeless youth enjoy living in the streets without rules," says Ken Cowdery, executive director of New Avenues for Youth in Portland, Oregon. "The vast majority of kids we deal with are victims of severe abuse—smart runaways escaping dangerous situations."

A 2003 study by the Center for Law and Social Policy [CLASP] found that half of the homeless youth interviewed reported "intense conflict or physical harm by a family member." Other studies back that up. "Wherever I Can Lay My Head: Homeless Youth on Homelessness," a 2005 study issued by Chicago's Department of Children and Youth Services and The Night Ministry, reports that instances of emotional or physical abuse by family members were greater than 50 percent. It also found that 36 percent of homeless girls and almost 14 percent of boys were sexually abused at home.

Experts point out that many homeless kids don't run away at all. As opposed to runaways, "thowaways" are kids who have been kicked out of the house, slowly driven out, or abandoned by their parents. The CLASP study found that 62 percent of the homeless youth interviewed said that a member of their family or household had let them know they were no longer wanted.

The reasons kids find themselves homeless and alone are many. Like Aaron Bowen, lots of teenagers end up on the street because of familial conflict concerning sexual orientation. In the Chicago study, 13.5 percent cited sexual orientation as a factor that led to homelessness. One 17-year-old transgender youth quoted in the study reveals just how stark family life for a LGBTQ (lesbian, gay, bisexual, transgender, questioning) youth can be: "[My] parents moved away without me."

Many other conflicts that contribute to homelessness have to do with teen pregnancy or parenting—11 percent and six percent, respectively, according to the study. Drug and alcohol abuse—both by teens and their parents—is also frequently a contributing factor to youth homelessness, as are issues of mental health.

A family history of homelessness, unstable housing, or economic crises may also lead to youth homelessness. A 2004 U.S. Conference of Mayors study of 27 major cities found that families with children accounted for 50 percent of the urban homeless population, and that population is thought to be larger in rural areas. The study noted that while shelter capacity for families increased in 2004, about one-third of requests for shelter were denied that year. Complicating matters for teens, particularly boys, is that finding shelter often means splitting up the family. Men and boys (sometimes as young as 10) are frequently not allowed in shelters that also serve women and children.

Other homeless youth come out of the foster care system, having either run away from foster parents and group homes or having "aged out" (generally at age 18, but at 21 in some states) from the system. Minors who haven't been emancipated can receive substantial help only from within the child welfare system—the law obliges care providers to report them and turn them over.

Still others are kids released from the juvenile justice system who refuse to go home or don't have a family to go back to. The list goes on. . . .

Without a Home

At the root of teen homelessness, just as it is for adults and families, is a chronic, well-documented affordable housing shortage. (A March 2006 study of rental housing by the Joint Center for Housing Studies and Harvard University added to the volume of literature on the topic. It found that although 100,000 affordable rental units were built in the U.S. every year, 200,000 were torn down.)

"[Youth] have the additional barrier of not being old enough to sign a lease, for instance," explains Nan Roman, president of the National Alliance to End Homelessness. "Issues having to do with their age make it more difficult, but housing affordability is certainly the driver."

In the past, cities, states, and the federal government have largely adopted policies aimed at managing the problem of homelessness. Emergency shelters, food pantries, job training, substance abuse clinics, mental health programs, and other programs sought to help stabilize homeless and at-risk people, on the assumption that a more stable life would make finding and keeping permanent housing more feasible.

That's changing, however. Today's efforts are centered around "housing first," with the idea that only when someone is in a safe, reliable place can they begin to work on other life issues. The housing first model is problematic, however, for unaccompanied young people.

"While we have a clear path for ending homelessness among adults, this path might not be quite as clear for youth," says Roman. "They need housing and they need support. And they often need housing in a different way."

She notes that their general lack of education and experience—with living on their own, engaging in various social situations and with the larger community, and working— makes the needs of teens very different from those of adults. And long-term, so-called "permanent" housing doesn't suit homeless teens as well as it might older homeless individuals.

Young people by nature are a fairly mobile group, and it's unrealistic to expect an 18-year-old to want to stay put in one apartment for a year, let alone a decade, Roman notes.

"As in so many realms, we're just not adequately attending to the housing needs of young people who are vulnerable," Roman says.

Where to Go?

Homeless kids who seek help are likely to make first contact at a youth shelter or through an outreach program that sends staff and volunteers into the streets to give out food, clothing, and counseling, as well as information on shelters, medical treatment, and other services. At a shelter, staff will first try to reunite a homeless youth with his or her family or a relative—if safe and appropriate—or contact child welfare if the teen is a ward of the state.

Then—if the kid doesn't go back to the streets—they work towards whatever longer term placement is appropriate, because homeless kids can't stay in a shelter forever.

Indeed, shelter care has its limitations. Under the 1974 federal Runaway and Homeless Youth Act [RHYA], which helps fund local nonprofits that serve runaway, homeless, missing, and sexually exploited children, basic centers (emergency shelters) offer residential care for up to 15 days, as well as providing meals, clothing, and medical care (or access to such care); counseling; and after-care services. The staffs seek to reunite youth with family—if possible—or find alternative placements with relatives, foster care, or in family-style group homes. While for some, making contact with these shelters may be the first step towards ending homelessness, many drop in for a day or a week before moving on. Then the cycle repeats.

In Transition

The idea is to get kids into a normal setting—or at least work toward it. For younger kids, that often means a family-like set-

Victoria Rowell Is a Foster Care Success Story

Film and television star Victoria Rowell works diligently to raise awareness about the issues surrounding foster care. . . .

Victoria entered the Maine foster care system as an infant, and lived in a number of homes with nurturing foster parents who helped identify her talents and shape her future career.

At the age of sixteen, after eight years of formal training, Victoria received scholarships to the School of American Ballet and American Ballet Theater in New York City. After a series of tours with Ballet Hispanico, the Julliard School of Music and Twyla Tharp Workshops, Victoria began her modeling and acting career.

"Success Stories: Victoria Rowell," www.fostercaremonth.com.

ting with foster parents or in a group home. For older kids, the best option is often a transitional living program, which helps them acquire the know-how to live self-sufficiently so that they can eventually get and keep permanent housing on their own.

"Normal" for the vast majority of young people just starting out includes relying on financial support from family members, if needed. Parents also help their young adult children look for apartments, negotiate leases, and deal with other unfamiliar tasks. Homeless kids have no such familial support, and that makes finding and keeping conventional housing very difficult.

The transitional living programs that receive funding from RHYA last as long as 18 months (sometimes longer for teens under 18). Living accommodations may vary—from group homes to market-rate apartments—but all programs offer a mix of training in life skills (such as budgeting and parenting), interpersonal skills, and job skills, as well as traditional educational opportunities such as GED [general educational development] programs and alternative high schools. When employment becomes stable, youth are expected to contribute a fixed amount or a percentage of their income towards housing costs.

Lighthouse Youth Services in Cincinnati opened its Lighthouse Runaway Shelter (now called the Youth Crisis Center) in 1974, and was one of the first recipients of funding under RHYA and the only youth shelter in the area. Each year, the 24-bed facility serves 1,500 children ages 10 through 17—even if some have to sleep on cots, says Bob Mecum, president and CEO. Lighthouse has had success getting younger teens into foster homes, and eventually, a third of them get adopted, he notes.

Early on, however, Mecum saw a huge gap in care for kids 18 and up. "As we learned more about the adult shelter care facilities, we began to realize how many older youth were going into these adult shelters and really not doing well," Mecum says. "These 18-, 19-, and 20-year-olds were so remarkably different than the older, stereotypical homeless adult with mental health problems, addiction," and chronic homelessness.

"And adult shelters were having a hard time," he adds. "[Young adults] were coming in with behavioral issues—fighting, aggressive behavior, neediness. Adult shelters had trouble engaging them and some were being preyed upon by older adults."

In 1989, Lighthouse began operating its Transitional Living Program. Initially, to receive HUD funding, Mecum says, the program had to focus on housing; it placed young adults in buildings that the agency owned—similar to permanent housing solutions for adults. At one point, the agency owned four such apartment buildings where teens would live, with supervision, as they learned independent living skills, finished their education, and learned how to get a job.

Today, the program continues, but with fewer agency-owned buildings. Mecum notes that about 90 youth currently live in leased, scattered-site apartments in the community, thanks in part to a shift in HDD's funding model.

Mecum sees a place for both models, depending on the person. "The most ideal aspect of the scattered-site model," he says, "is that you can not only put them in a location that makes sense for the person, near work or school, for instance, but also turn the apartment over to them if the person is able to get a job and learn how to keep the apartment. Even as they get older, they don't have to leave."

Matt Schnars likes the scattered-site model as well. Schnars, the independent living program director at Haven House Services in Raleigh, North Carolina, works with teens aged 16 to 21; 75 percent of them enter his program at 18 or 19. "Many have been involved with programs [such as Haven House's group foster homes], have been in foster care, the juvenile justice system, or mental health group homes," he says. "They haven't had the support to transition out into the community and they have no idea what it takes to go out and obtain housing. Some are functioning on a 5th or 6th grade reading level—they don't have the skills to get a job or negotiate with a landlord."

Transitional and semi-independent living programs allow young adults to learn those things and put them into practice, while still giving them a safety net. "They may find themselves in totally unfamiliar territory—in middle-class society where the survival skills from their street life don't apply," Schnars says. "Being out of their element, there's a natural fear of failure."

Schnars tells the story of one young woman who called in a panic because she had just gotten paid and didn't know what to do with her check. "She wanted help getting her money put away before she blew it," he says. "They're aware of their vulnerability," he adds.

Two in One

Chicago's Night Ministry handles transitional housing a little differently. It just opened a new facility that accommodates its 120-day interim housing program, which has served about 200 youth ranging in age from 14 to 21 (and their young children) annually since opening in 1992.

As its name implies, the interim program is "smack dab in the middle" of the care spectrum, Maguire says. Youth may stay longer than they would in an emergency shelter—and receive the support they need—while they prepare for the next step towards solving their homelessness. At the dorm-style Open Door Shelter, two teens share a room that has been carefully fitted with furniture, rugs, and linens that say "home" rather than "institution." The residents attend school or work during the day and participate in life-skill classes, counseling sessions, job-skill training, and other group and individual activities at night.

The average stay in the four-month program is 30 to 40 days, and Maguire says she sees youth, particularly older youth, come back two and three times. "Would we like them to stay 120 days? Yes. But they get excited and want to fly out on their own."

For those not quite ready to fly, the new facility also offers two transitional living apartments on the top floor, where eight young men and women, and their infants or toddlers, can live for one to two years while practicing independent living skills.

Residents of the apartments each have a case manager who helps them learn the skills to become self-sufficient, but the youth have more autonomy, personal space, and responsibility than residents of the interim program. Maguire expects that some youth who move up to the apartments may realize they're not quite ready yet, and may move back downstairs into the interim program. And that's perfectly O.K.

Keeping Tabs

The Homeless Youth System in Portland, Oregon, is often cited for its efficiency, effectiveness, and level of collaboration with other homeless service providers, mental and physical health professionals, and even the police. (When cops pick up teens for minor offenses, they're not taken to a juvenile detention center but to the reception center, which gets in touch with the family and offers counseling and access to other services.)

Together, three organizations—New Avenues for Youth, Janus Youth Programs, and Outside In—operate an intake center, shelters, day services centers (for meals, showers, storage facilities), drug and alcohol treatment programs, an alternative high school, a medical clinic, and transitional and independent housing.

The youth system is also part of a sophisticated data management system. New Avenues for Youth's Ken Cowdery says that people come from all over the country, as well as places such as Mexico, New Zealand, and China, asking, "How did you do this?" "I tell them this," Cowdery says. "People were frustrated with the lack of coordination. Add to that a great deal of compassion and a lot of smart people in government who know how to get things done and who knew it was important to have a unified database."

That database not only gives New Avenues easy-to-use data, but it also provides reliable information to governments and private donors, as well as to the media (which is credited in Portland for having helped to publicize and demand action on the city's homelessness problems).

All agencies collect data about the people they serve, but, says Heather Lyons, homeless program manager for the Portland Bureau of Housing and Development, Portland's model is different because it allows various service providers to share information. It opens up the silos of service to create a more collaborative atmosphere of care. The system-wide Homeless Managemanent Information System [HMIS] is being implemented, in part, in response to a 2004 congressional mandate that recipients of HUD's Continuum of Care homelessness lands participate in an HMIS.

"But ours goes beyond the federal mandate, touching services for low-income or at-risk populations, people with chemical dependence problems," and other groups that aren't necessarily—but may be—homeless, Lyons notes. (Congress has also laid out a plan to better track kids exiting the foster care system, but the Youth in Transition Database hasn't yet been implemented.)

Homeward Bound

One formerly homeless young woman in Portland offered her gratitude in a letter to New Avenues for Youth. "I know that when I'm older and when my life is more stabel [sic] my time will be a more appropriate way of showing my thanks," she wrote. "For now my words are all I have to give."

Because of the various programs and people looking out for them, she and a lot of other teens across the U.S. will lay down their heads tonight—and the next night—in a safe place. It may not be what most people envision when they think of home, but it might be better than the car, abandoned building, lumpy couch of a friend of a friend, or highway underpass that these youths may have called "home" shortly before.

For Aaron Bowen, who's living in an SRO in Chicago, working, and heading up PACT's homeless team, things are definitely looking up, but not altogether rosy. "I got robbed last Wednesday," he told me when we talked in early April.

But the young man, who says he has been a youth advocate since he was 15, feels passionately about his role and that of other formerly homeless youth in combating youth home-lessness—which is why he shares his story.

| "The largest driver of the young adult homeless population is the foster care system."

Older Teens Cycle Out of Foster Care and Return to the Streets

Carol Smith

Two dynamics are forcing young adults onto the streets—the failure of the foster care system and a cycle of homelessness that began when their parents became crack addicts in the 1980s—according to Carol Smith in the following viewpoint. Young adults leave the foster care system when they turn 18. Research shows that one in five of these young people will be homeless within two years. Solutions to this problem include finding appropriate housing for these young adults and providing job training that will enable them to get jobs at a decent wage, maintains the author. Carol Smith is an investigative reporter for the Seattle PostGlobe.

As you read, consider the following questions:

1. What incentive for becoming pregnant does the executive director of ROOTS identify, according to the author?

2. What does the author cite as the unemployment rate for young adults?

3. What is the increase in the number of youths "aging out" of the foster care system, according to the author?

Shelters for young adults in King County are turning people away in record numbers as unemployment escalates and housing costs continue to be out of reach. This surge in demand for shelter reveals a new face of homelessness, one fueled by the legacy of a failing foster care system and young people stranded by the crack epidemic of the late 1980s.

Some of those young people are now having families of their own, and without resources, are winding up homeless. Families are the fastest-growing segment of the homeless population. Yet the group driving this trend—young adults ages 18–24—is generally under-counted and under-represented when solutions are envisioned. Relatively few resources are being directed to prevent them from producing new generations of homeless families.

One of the most disturbing legacies of homelessness is that it can be handed down from parent to child. Children who experience homelessness growing up are more likely to experience it as adults.

Casi Jackson is part of the problem, and part of the solution. At work at a homeless outreach center on Seattle's Eastside, she shifts her daughter, Tiana, 7 months, on her hip and juggles a cell phone in her other hand while she fields a call from a scared-sounding mom with no place to sleep tonight. Slender, with long curly hair, and an unflinching manner,

Jackson is matter-of-fact on the phone, and sounds older than her 22 years. She knows what it's like to be staring down a night without shelter.

Homeless families are typically headed by young women with young children.

Jackson was homeless at 20. She had borne three children by 21. One died. One is now living with a grandparent. One lives with her. She has another on the way as she struggles to make for them what she never had—a stable home with a family under one roof.

Jackson clicks off the call in the bare cubicle that serves as a makeshift office for Vets Edge, the grassroots homeless outreach service run by her friend and mentor Joe Ingram out of the front lobby of the Together Center, a campus of 16 nonprofits in downtown Redmond [Washington state]. Tiana clambers to get down, and Jackson holds her daughter's hands while the baby wobbles to her feet.

Chaos

Good counts are hard to come by, but some estimate up to 2 million young people become homeless nationwide each year. In King County, an estimated 1,000 young people are homeless on any given night.

It's a group driven by two large converging forces—an economy that has been especially brutal on young people, and the large numbers currently "aging out" or growing to adulthood in foster care.

While King County's one-night count showed an overall decrease of 5 percent in the total numbers of homeless, shelters for young adults are turning people away in record numbers, said Kristine Cunningham, executive director of ROOTS in Seattle, one of the pioneering young adult shelters in the country.

ROOTS expects to have to turn away young people 2,000 times this year, compared with 200 times five years ago, said

Cunningham, and that's even as the number of shelter beds for young adults in Seattle has increased. "The odds of getting a bed are about one in seven."

"We've Incentivized Becoming Pregnant"

For some of those young people, getting pregnant is perceived as a way out of homelessness. There's a perception on the street that if you're about to give birth, you can get housing, said Cunningham. "We've incentivized becoming pregnant." Wait lists are just as burdened for housing for young families, but having a child does make a young person eligible for services not available to childless young adults.

So homelessness becomes a self-perpetuating problem.

Children born to homeless mothers, or who experience multiple episodes of housing instability—couch surfing, staying in motels, or shuttling between households when they are young—often mirror that in their own adulthoods.

Jackson's own trajectory shows how homelessness can pass from generation to generation. She was born in a California jail. Her military father was deployed when his baby daughter was discharged from the jail medical ward.

She spent her childhood knocking between relatives, most often with a grandmother, a foster parent who was also raising many of Jackson's cousins.

"If I had to characterize my childhood in one word," she said, "it would be chaos."

Priced Out

Young people age 18 to 24 make up 26 percent of homeless families.

Yet, of all segments of the homeless population, young adults probably receive the least attention, have the fewest resources applied to help them, and have the least amount of policy advocacy on their behalf, said Mark Putnam, a lead consultant for Building Changes, a nonprofit focused on ending homelessness. "There's not a coalition for them in Washington state," he said. At the national level, it's barely on the radar of the National Alliance to End Homelessness, a powerful advocacy group that provides information the U.S. Department of Housing and Urban Development.

"Being homeless is like a picture of someone screaming, and no one coming to help," said Tony Torres, 22, a former foster kid who spent the last four years on the street, in and out of shelters and has just now gotten a temporary bed in a transitional home.

Shane Thomas, 23, is one of an estimated 1,000 young adults believed homeless nightly in Seattle. He picks up jobs on fishing boats when he can, but despite the seasonal, temporary gigs, he still winds up staying on the street and in shelters.

"The thing about being homeless—you get stuck in one spot," he said. "Might get a little more money in your pocket the next day, but you're still going to be broke."

There's a cultural bias that these young people are ablebodied, and should be working, Putnam said. "People prejudge they made a choice to be on the street."

For most, it's not a choice.

Making it on your own at age 18 may have been possible for their parents' generation, said Rachel Antrobus, director of San-Francisco based Transitional Age Youth Initiative, an agency that works to coordinate services for 18- to 24-year-olds. "But that's not actually a reality anymore."

Unemployment rates are higher among young adults than other age groups. In July [2010], the youth unemployment rate edged over 19 percent, the highest July rate on record since 1948.

"The 30-year-olds are taking jobs from 20-year-olds, because the 40-year-olds are taking the 30-year-old's jobs," said Putnam. "These guys are truly employment victims of the recession."

Those that used to get by sharing a studio with someone else, or moving back in with their folks, can't even make that happen anymore.

Nationally, a wage-earner in a family with children has to make almost $18 an hour to afford the average two-bedroom apartment. In King County, families must earn 2-1/2 times the minimum wage of $8.55 an hour, or $21.40, to afford even a modest two-bedroom apartment.

That's out of reach for many young adults, especially those with limited education and training.

Curtis, 24, who didn't want his last name used, wound up staying at The Landing, a young adult shelter in Bellevue, after the place he was renting went into foreclosure. He hasn't been able to scrape together enough money to find a new place on his wages parking cars for a luxury hotel. "Some places are asking like $1500 to 2 grand for deposit," he said. "The whole situation just really sucks."

From Foster Care to the Streets

The economy, however, only compounds an even larger underlying problem: The largest driver of the young adult homeless population is the foster care system.

"Once you hit 18, you get dumped from the system and forgotten about," said Torres, who lived in multiple foster homes from the age of 12 until he was 18. He suffers from kidney failure, and has had to juggle difficult medical treatments with life on the streets.

At age 18, states stop providing money for support of foster children.

The Mockingbird Society, a foster youth advocacy group based in Seattle, lobbied successfully to get federal legislation passed to extend support until age 21. The Fostering Connections to Success Act passed in 2008 provides federal matching funds for extending foster support. But the fight now is to get states to put up their part of the money, said spokeswoman

Rose Berg. There's a law, but so far, few states have financed programs that would qualify to get the match.

Shut out of jobs for lack of training, priced out of housing for lack of jobs, they also lack family support that can bridge the tough times.

In 2009, 80 percent of college graduates moved home after finishing school, according to job listing web site Collegegrad-.com, up from 77 percent in 2008 and 67 percent in 2006. Those without the training and family support of college graduates are hurting even more.

About 80 percent of those staying at The Landing, the Bellevue shelter for young adults, have been in foster care, said Denise Wallace, mental health counselor at shelter.

Nationally, a report by Pew Charitable Trusts showed while the number of kids in foster care has been declining, the number of those aging out is on the rise, increasing by 41 percent between 1998 and 2005. About 20,000 young people a year age out of foster care.

This is the legacy of the crack epidemic of the 1980s, said Antrobus. Many of the kids who have been aging out went into the system as a byproduct of that era of rampant drug use by their parents. "We've been in a peak for a few years, and we will be for a few more."

Studies, including those done by Pew, also show that one in five of those who age out will be homeless within two years of leaving foster care. Half won't have a high school degree. Less than 3 percent graduate college. A 2004 study by Casey Family Programs in conjunction with Washington's Department Social and Health Services [DSHS] showed 13 percent of those leaving foster care in this state became homeless within a year and more than half were unemployed.

By the time they age out of foster care at age 18, 20 percent of young women are already parents themselves. Another 40 percent are pregnant.

Foster Care Failed Cindy

Shortly after her 18th birthday, Cindy (not her real name) left her group home in the Bronx to live with her mother. Although under New York laws she could have stayed in the foster care system until she turned 21, Cindy had lived in foster homes and group homes for nearly six years, and she was eager to move on. Still, she was apprehensive about living at home again. Her fears were well-founded. Cindy and her mother argued and she soon found herself on the street. Cindy has now been homeless for several months, bouncing between Covenant House and her boyfriend's apartment. Her boyfriend sometimes hits her, but she feels she can't leave him because she depends on him for survival—food, shelter, even emotional support. She doesn't see any way out.

Kendra Hurley, "Almost Home,"
NHI Shelterforce Online, September/October 2002.

"We're seeing a lot of kids who have been in foster care, their kids are now in foster care," said Julie Jacobson, director of the Center for Young Adults at the Seattle YMCA.

Broken Families

Jackson first got pregnant when she was 18. She moved to Seattle, and was living with her boyfriend and his mother when, she says, the relationship turned violent.

Her boyfriend hit her when she was pregnant with their second, she said. That baby was born prematurely at 25 weeks, not quite 2 pounds. He died of pneumonia just a few weeks after coming home. Scared and deeply depressed, she fled through a bedroom window in the middle of the night.

Homeless with her 18-month-old daughter in tow, she couldn't immediately find a shelter that would take her with a baby. Friends helped, but she eventually wound up at Harborview Medical Center in desperation. Harborview called Child Protective Services, and Jackson agreed to give temporary custody of her daughter to the child's paternal grandmother, a crisis decision she says she now regrets.

That episode of homelessness broke apart her family. A pro-bono lawyer who specializes in helping former foster children is helping her try to reunify. But it's moving slowly. And she's acutely aware of the potential effects on her daughter.

"I moved around as a kid from home to home. I know it's hard to do," she said. "I don't want to do that to her."

Garbage Bag Kids

Homelessness begets homelessness.

People who don't grow up with stable homes don't develop many of the coping strategies that let them transition into stable home lives as adults, said Cunningham of ROOTS.

Some lack practical life skills as well. Many don't drive because the state restricts foster parents from teaching them. Many don't have conflict-resolution skills that it takes to survive in a workplace.

Their coping strategies are for surviving the street. People on the street use drugs the same way people with houses use TV, said Torres, the former foster child who became homeless. "To escape." They fight and steal when they have to. They do what they need to do to stay alive.

"And when something happens," Cunningham said, "it's easier to just run."

Cunningham, who formerly worked for DSHS, used to drive the "garbage bag" car on the day multiple foster children played musical houses. "All their possessions would be in that garbage bag," she said.

But those kids carry other baggage as well. Educational delays, shame, and a pervasive sense of being unwanted. Many have been abused.

"There's a lot of trauma," said Wallace, the counselor who works at The Landing.

A University of Washington study found that foster youth have nearly twice the rate of PTSD [Post-traumatic stress disorder] as war veterans.

Many have also absorbed negative impressions about their own potential and capabilities.

"There's a stigma attached to being 17 and in the tenth grade," said Jacobson. "No one sits with them and says, 'What are your hopes and dreams?'"

Losing Everything

Jackson does have hopes and dreams. And they came with getting a roof over her head.

She wants, first, to get her daughter back. She wants to get her degree in social work from the University of Washington. She wants to work as a peer counselor for other women who have lost children as a result of domestic violence.

For Jackson, and others like her, getting housing is like winning a lottery.

It is, in fact, a lottery. Jackson was on three wait lists for subsidized transitional housing when she lucked out and got a Section 8 voucher.

That voucher enabled her to move to her apartment and start to straighten out her life without the typical two-year wait. Maintaining housing, however, is also something of a lottery.

"Honestly, it's something I think about all the time—when am I going to be homeless again? I'm scared of losing it all. I always wonder—what if Section 8 runs out of money. What if my program goes under? I know that when I was homeless last time, I lost everything." Jackson is standing in the middle of her living room, apologizing for the mess. It's June, and her pregnancy has started to show.

"I don't have nice things because I would just lose them all again," she said.

But she does have the things that are most important to her. She has two harmless corn snakes in an aquarium—pets she's had since she was a young teen. She has an antique sewing machine given to her by another person about to become homeless.

"She wanted it to go to someone who wouldn't throw it away," she said. She has her deceased son's footprints in clay.

The last time she saw her older daughter was two months ago. Regular visits are difficult to arrange. It takes three buses and three hours to reach the city where she lives. And she's not able to see her at the grandparent's home because she has a no contact order against the child's father, and there's always a possibility he will be there.

"I'm sick of not seeing my daughter," she said. "I'm just trying to do this the right way."

Solutions

The young adult segment of the homeless population has unique needs and challenges that so far have not been well addressed, say those who work with this population.

Seattle and San Francisco are ahead of the curve in providing specialized emergency shelter for this demographic. In many other cities, young people have to go to general adult shelters, or sleep outside.

"Even though it's not age appropriate to be with older shelter population, at this time, we don't have a separate option," said Josephine Pufpaff, director of Youth Link in Minneapolis, which tries to help young people transitioning to adulthood.

While other programs that aid homeless families focus on preventing evictions or foreclosures, for example, the issue facing many young homeless adults is getting into housing in the first place.

Ruth Blaw, director of the Orion Center, a drop-in center for young adults, said there are long wait lists for housing. "It could be six months," she said. "Or it could be forever."

And when the lucky few do get housing, they sometimes lose it because they aren't prepared to fit into it.

"The approaches we've tried are not working," said Cunningham. Young people who have been on the street often don't fit well into existing models of group housing where many young people share small common areas and are required to live under strict rules. She suggests a model that allows them more independence, while still providing support service, such as job training and counseling, would be more successful.

There's also a need for more job training geared at getting real, living wage jobs, said Putnam.

More than half of foster youth remain unemployed within a year of turning 19, more than double their rate of their peers overall. And of the remaining foster youth who do-work, half were working at sub-poverty or minimum-wage jobs.

In fact, many of the young people using both The Landing and ROOTS have minimum wage jobs working at fast-food restaurants and other places, but still can't make enough to get into places of their own.

Two Doors

Jackson's baby is due any day now, and she's excited. She's been paring down the clutter in her apartment, clearing the living room so her baby and friends' children can play.

This new baby will be a boy. A social worker from Healthy Start, who has been working with her since Tiana was born, has been helping her prepare.

She's seeking financial aid to complete her associate's degree at Bellevue College. She's making new friends—friends who aren't homeless. She and the baby's father, who is in her life, are trying to make plans for the future.

Jackson perches Tiana on the shelf of her belly while she tends to her friend's crying two-year-old.

"You want to play with this?" she asks them. She zips open a pop-up house, a nylon, tent-like contraption that springs into shape taking up most of the small living room.

Both children crow with glee and tumble in.

The phone rings. It's Ingram, her outreach director. Another new family is asking for help. The two of them have handled twice as many calls this year as last. In this economy, young families who are housed one moment, can be homeless the next. It never gets easier to find them help.

Jackson puts the phone down and watches the children. They giggle and roll on the floor of the toy house. They stretch to try to touch the ceiling.

"They love this thing," she says. "It has two doors.

"They can go in and out. Either side."

> *"Although these youth had run from or been abandoned by their families of origin, they had not, in fact, abandoned the cultural idea of a family unit."*

Street Families Can Make Street Teens Safer

Joanne O'Sullivan Oliveira and Pamela J. Burke

Street families have been shown to provide street teens with the support that traditional families generally give children—protecting them against danger, supplying food, and giving them a sense of belonging and security, according to Joanne O'Sullivan Oliveira and Pamela J. Burke. In their study of nineteen street teens who were part of a street family around an area called the "Pit" in Cambridge, Massachusetts, they conclude that teens can find in a street family what they are missing at home and reconnect to society. Oliveira is director of surgical programs at Children's Hospital, Boston. Pamela J. Burke is a nurse practitioner in the Division of Adolescent Medicine, and co-director for nurse training at Children's Hospital, Boston, and assistant professor of pediatrics at Harvard Medical School.

Joanne O'Sullivan Oliveira and Pamela J. Burke, "Lost in the Shuffle: Culture of Homeless Adolescents," *Pediatric Nursing*, vol. 35, no. 3, May–June, 2009, pp. 154–61.

As you read, consider the following questions:

1. How do the authors define culture?

2. According to street family member Bam-Bam as quoted by the authors, what is the attraction of Wicca to the community around the "Pit" in Cambridge?

3. What are the positive aspects of street families that the authors found in their interviews?

Every culture has a schema, which can be expressed as family structure; dietary habits; religious practices; the development of art, music, and drama; ways of communicating; dress; and health behavior. Literature on runaway adolescents dates back to the 1920s, but very little research focuses on the culture of homeless adolescents. Homeless adolescents exist literally on the periphery of society, often leading to exclusion and marginalization, as these youth gravitate toward isolated locations, such as abandoned areas of the city, hidden spaces in public buildings, and remote or inaccessible sites. Ultimately, they find themselves prohibited from participating in society and limited in their use of societal powers and resources. This study explores the culture and life experiences of homeless adolescents in a major urban area. . . .

Relationship Dynamics

Much of the existing research on homeless adolescents has focused on the epidemiology [the study of diseases affecting a large population] of homelessness, precipitating factors, and perspectives of service providers. However, what is not well understood is the youth's perspective of life on the streets and the dynamic relationships that homeless youth form for survival. Previous research has focused intently on the problems and deficits of homeless adolescents, with little or no attention to the strengths and competencies these youth possess. Research is needed to explore the subculture of homelessness as experienced by the adolescents and described from their own perspective.

The aims of this doctoral dissertation study were to 1) explore the meaning of life for homeless adolescents, 2) examine how these youth structure their lives and how society has helped create that structure, 3) describe the cultural norms and mores of street life, and 4) understand how social, economic, and political forces within mainstream culture may influence the formation of a homeless adolescent subculture. The most appropriate study design to meet this study's aims was ethnography [close observation of a culture]. . . .

Culture can be defined as a set of guidelines that individuals inherit as members of a particular society. According to [J.P.] Spradley, when ethnographers study other cultures, they must deal with what people do (cultural behavior), what people know (cultural knowledge), and what people make (cultural artifacts). The elements of the street culture of homeless adolescents were identified by the study participants' stories.

Environment

Typically, homeless youth found one another at the *Pit*, a Mecca to homeless youth. This sunken plaza was adjacent to the subway stop across from a major university [Harvard University]. A variety of individuals could be found at the Pit, including musicians, rebellious teens (with and without homes), students, and tourists. The environment provided a cultural center and a place to belong.

Cultures are made up of customs, mores, and ethos that are based on a belief system. The roots of these youth were grounded in the practice of Wicca. The ritualistic religion of Wicca emerged in almost every participant's interview. Religion, particularly Wicca (a pre-Christian pagan religion), was one of the strongest threads holding these street youth together. Wicca's major influence was on the rules of conduct and ethics of their culture. These youth felt a connection with pagan rituals that were inclusive and provided a sense of family and community. Experienced members tutored those who were new to the streets in the ways of Wicca. This became an important bonding process and a factor in whether the new member would be accepted into the street family.

For Bam-Bam, as for many others living on the street, religion (whether mainstream or alternative) played a significant role in homeless "family" ties. Bam-Bam stated he had been practicing Wicca for over 8 years. In presenting a portrait of Bam-Bam, the practice of Wicca was reported as a central component to the structure of the subculture of these homeless adolescents. Divorced from families of origin and mainstream society, these youth have foraged for a sense of structure and organization. Bam-Bam's religious beliefs in Wicca, as with many of his fellow homeless adolescents, provide a mirror into this culture. Quoting Bam-Bam:

> There is a large community around the "Pit," and many of the members in the "Pit" are part of one joint community family. Our family is Wicca/Pagan. We have our parents. We have kids. We have aunts and uncles. Being Pagan, our family is definitely differed from most other families. Most of us in the family believe that we have been around for many centuries on earth or whatever people want to call it, this planet, this rock. You have to be part of our energy circle where we transfer energy between one another. Then we will fill you in on some history of our family.

> Wicca is an old Celtic religion, which took on New Age philosophies in the 1980s. We all have been around for a long time. We have a high council of members of the family that have been in the family the longest, that know all the functions around the family, the rules of the family. How things are supposed to be done the right way and on council, where I'm the eldest son. So I am next in line to help protect my family. We all like to protect each other, make sure everybody is safe at all times. There are always other members in the family around at all times if there's ever an emergency or something like that.

On the street, most come to Wicca because it means family, community, and commitment. Wicca beliefs and practices arose from a sense of community just like the street family, within the early clans. To "go it alone" was not a traditional Wicca value. We believe in following our own intuition and own personal code of ethics and morality. Wiccas look within, perceiving themselves to be both student and teacher at the same time. A lot of it is street family, but we tie in Wicca. Most of the family members are Wicca.

We have one member, the newest member of the family; she's fairly new to the Wicca and Pagan religion. . . we are slowly bringing her in and letting her know what is going on. We are doing it so it is not overwhelming or scary. We are just slowly showing her this is what happens. I feel that in some way, everybody is Wicca or Pagan because there is always energy transferred no matter what, human or inhuman.

Street Families

Although these youth had run from or been abandoned by their families of origin, they had not, in fact, abandoned the cultural ideal of a family unit. To survive on the streets, they formed new street families complete with pseudo parents, siblings, and other extended family relationships. A street Mom and Dad in their 30s and former homeless youth helped scout out squats for sleeping and were instrumental in resolving conflicts. In this street family unit, there were two family factions headed by elder sons who were designated because of their length of time living on the streets. Bam-Bam and Casper were regarded as elders and initiated new homeless youth into the family. These street families provided the homeless youth with the resources and social support needed to survive the danger, boredom, poverty, challenges, and frustrations inherent in their transient and fragile existence.

"The best thing that has happened to me since I began life on the streets is the making of my street family" (Jade, female).

During each interview, a repetitive theme surfaced about life on the streets and the formation of "street families." What most professionals would regard as a negative experience was described positively by many of these youth. The adolescents had either run from or been abandoned by their original families. This left a void in their need for family ties. Their street families took alternate forms, as evidenced by both Bam-Bam's and Jade's accounts, and for these vulnerable youngsters, such ties were as important as food and water. These youth felt they finally belonged because they had established a family bond and found unconditional acceptance. They now had a family upon which they could depend, and this generated feelings of security. Some of these youth stated this was the first time in their lives they could "act like a kid," while others said they were discovering their lost childhood and finally felt part of a family, a community, a society, and a culture. . . .

Freedom and Danger

Findings revealed that homeless adolescents fashioned a defined culture of unprecedented freedom and baffling complexity that is neither seen nor imagined by mainstream society. It is a culture with rules but little structure, with values but questionable morality, and with codes but not much consistency. Although street life may generate social capital, it can also be dangerous because of youth's engagement in multiple risk activities, such as drug use and survival sex. . . .

The youth in this study felt better cared for on the streets than at home because of the camaraderie and nurturing within their subculture. Therefore, they were not necessarily opting to be homeless per se, but were selecting a safer and more welcoming environment. The street community offered tangible support through shared resources, such as food, shelter, money, and other basic necessities.

These homeless adolescents also formed nationwide networks that they referred to as a community or family, and whose members were cultivated through Internet communication. They accessed the Internet via computers at public libraries or social service centers, exchanging email addresses and communicating with each other as they traveled across the country. They sought out companionship and acceptance from other youth who came from similar backgrounds, and this spawned a sense of belonging to this street family culture. The more these youth felt embraced by their street family, the longer they remained on the streets.

> *"One out of four street family members in [a] study admitted to crimes that qualified as attempted murder."*

Street Families Can Make Street Teens More Violent

Rene Denfeld

The emergence in the late 1990s of a street family culture changed the culture of the street, according to Rene Denfeld in the following viewpoint. Prior to that time, street youth engaged in hedonistic behavior. With the emergence of street families and increased use of the drug methamphetamine, street youth have become more violent. Street families provide the framework for violent behavior by creating an atmosphere in which young people become increasingly alienated from society, retreating to a world of fantasy, the author suggests. Rene Denfeld is the author of The New Victorians *and has written for numerous publications, including the* New York Times. *She lives in Portland, Oregon.*

Rene Denfeld, *All God's Children: Inside the Dark and Violent World of Street Families.* New York: Public Affairs, 2007, pp. 59–69, 282–83. Copyright © 2007 by Rene Denfeld. All rights reserved. Reproduced by permission.

As you read, consider the following questions:

1. What reason do professors John Hagan and Bill McCarthy, as cited by the author, give for teens becoming more violent in street families?

2. According to the author, what has been responsible for the uniformity of street family culture across the United States?

3. What role do fantasy games have in encouraging violent behavior in street families, according to Denfeld?

In Portland, the first major street family came into being in 1998 with the Nihilistic Gutter Punks, or the NGP. The NGP made themselves a logo, which some members had tattooed on their bodies: an X with the letters "N," "G," and "P" in the upper three sprockets and the chaos star (a sun with arrows) underneath. At times they used two syringes crossing underneath a skull for the X. This was to signify methamphetamine use.

Street Families Became More Violent

The NGP family soon claimed between seventy and a hundred members. The family grew too large to squat together, and smaller families began to splinter off the main group. One of the first splinter families was a local chapter of the Sick Boys, which was formed in late December 1998, according to local street kids.

According to a street youth named Travis Harramen, a member of the Portland Sick Boys, the family originated in Orange County, California. Sick Boys is the name of a British punk band, as well as the name of a well-covered punk song by Social Distortion....

Other families rapidly appeared; including the 420s and the Portland Drunk Punks and even a group glorifying the murder of Michelle Woodall called the Fat Bitch Killers, whose members claimed to have murdered a "fat bitch in a wheelchair." Within a year, virtually all Portland-area street kids would claim to belong to one street family or another. Joining a family became a customary and expected part of living on the streets. The street kids also identified as Portland Street Kids, or PSK, in much the same way as a gang member might claim to be an Original Gangster but also a Crip or a Blood.

As the youths split into smaller factions, the families developed increasingly severe initiation rites. New members of the Sick Boys were beaten into the family and, at times, were told to inject eighty units (a large syringe) of methamphetamine into the neck, a shot that is now known as a Sick Boy. The female members of the Sick Boys were called Sick Bitches, and they had to commit assaults and robberies in order to earn the right to wear "Bitch Bangs," or the short fringe of hair that female street youths sometimes keep when they shave the rest of their hair off. If they wanted to tie objects in their Bitch Bangs, the Sick Bitches had to commit more assaults. The harsher the initiations, the more the street kids clamored to join, if only to prove how tough they were. One street kid was glowing after his initiation into a street family, despite the fact that he had a dislocated shoulder from the beating.

Until the arrival of the street families, Harramen says, most street kids had the simple common goal of "getting so drunk you puke on your shoes." The old street youth culture was built around getting drunk and getting laid. When fights broke out, the kids were usually too drunk to do much harm. Travis describes a sense of "unity" among the street kids, who were all enjoying drunken nihilism together. He believes two factors changed that drunken unity: methamphetamine and the street families. Travis went to prison himself in 2002 for blinding another street kid in an attack.

Perhaps as the inevitable result of the burgeoning families came what the street kids openly refer to as the 1999 "street wars." The street wars are virtually unknown outside the culture but had devastating impact on the street kids. "It got really, really bad, with fights and killings and attempted murders," Joshua Brown-Lenon, a Thantos Family member, says of the street wars. "Before the street wars, everyone was one big family," he claims. . . .

Street Families Teach Violence

Tempe, Arizona, a hot little desert town with a population of 158,000, is home to Arizona State University. In the 1990s, street families coalesced among the hundred or more street kids mingling on Mill Avenue alongside the university. The street kids liked Tempe for its warm, dry weather and the generosity of the local college students. Panhandling, they said, was especially lucrative.

In an extensive 1998 report for the *Phoenix New Times*, journalist David Holthouse followed a local street family called the Dank Krew, a play on the word *dank* (a kind of marijuana), as well as the smell of unwashed street youth. "Street kids in Tempe are almost all white, aged 14 to 26," he wrote. "A few grew up in the valley, the rest are from points across America. Most drink and smoke pot, and roughly half are junkies who picked up the needle once they were on the streets, not before. They call modern society 'Babylon.' A lot of them carry knives or bludgeons, and a few are dangerously violent."

Holthouse found that "violence is a near constant subtext among the street kids on Mill.". . .

Bart W. Miles, a professor of social work at Wayne State University in Detroit, Michigan, spent time with another Tempe street family called the Scum of Tempe, for his study "Street Life on Mill." The Scum family went by the usual street names, like Seven, Forty, Tweety, and Cowboy. Every weekend, as in other cities, the Scum of Tempe gathered with other street kids for a large drum circle, where they pounded on drums, sang, chanted, and smoked marijuana. Miles saw the drum circle as more than just entertainment for the youths. He believed it was a "major form of homeless identity," allowing the street kids to socialize and introduce new members to the culture. While the Scum family claimed to be less violent than other street families, they talked with ease about taking disobedient members "down to the tracks" and beating them up. For them, the lingo was "taking them off the streets."

In their 1999 study of street families, Canadian professors John Hagan and Bill McCarthy found that youths in street families are far more criminal than other homeless kids. One out of four street family members in their study admitted to crimes that qualified as attempted murder, such as attacking another person with a weapon with the intent to kill. Hagan and McCarthy say the reason is what they call *tutelage*. The street family acts as a mentor program, training and encouraging the street kids into violence, even murder. . . .

The Internet Spreads Family Culture

Of all the factors explaining how the street family culture became so consistent across the country, including the nomadic nature of the youths themselves, one influence has been overlooked: the Internet. The Internet has had a profound impact on the shaping and solidifying of what had been a transitory culture.

In the 1990s, street youth shelters began offering free computer access, and a number of Web sites either created by street kids or catering to them quickly appeared. The sites had names like road-dawgz.org, digihitch.com, hippy.com, and punkconnect.com. Street kids could enter a shelter and, within moments, be in touch with other street kids across the country. Aspects of street family culture from anarchist beliefs to squat rules became uniform from coast to coast. . . .

The Internet also became a recruitment tool. For instance, digihitch.com has a section devoted to sparkies, their term for

An Interview with Rene Denfeld on How She Became Interested in Street Families

How did you get interested in this topic [street families]?

It started in 1992 when I was living in a house in the lower Lair Hill area. We became aware of this group of street kids that were squatting under the Marquam Bridge, right down the street.

I became fascinated with them because they were so unlike the image of homeless youth that I'd had before. They were obviously organized into this little tribe; they squatted together, they hung out together, they panhandled together, and it turned out they committed a series of assaults and murders, as well.

They called themselves the family. And one of the people involved in that group went away to prison, James Daniel Nelson, and 11 years later he got out and murdered again. And that became the basis of this book.

Nick Budnick, "Street Life—and Death,"
Portland Tribune, *January 26, 2007.*

youths interested in the culture. Teenagers can post questions ranging from the best places to hitch to what kind of shoes to wear on the road. . . .

Fantasy Divorces Teens from Consequences

One can go to any American city and find street families talking about smiley chains and taxing, anarchy, dramas, and punishments. They will be squatting in similar squats and calling each other brother and sister, mother and father. They will be enforcing the same brand of ruthless street justice on each other and resisting all efforts to dislodge them from the streets, as scared and confused as they may be.

Not all will murder, just as not all gang members kill. But the groundwork is there. The dramas, the fantasy games these youths play outside the law, spiral all too easily into violence, and the codes they have created act like steps on a ladder leading them into further alienation from society. They are buffered from the consequences of their own violence until it is too late.

The outside world doesn't exist to these teenagers and young adults. With each taxing or assault, they become more entrenched in the fantasy life they have created. . . .

"Inside this world, this is normal," says Randy Blazak, an assistant professor of sociology and criminology at Portland State University and the coauthor of the 2001 book *Renegade Kids, Suburban Outlaws*. Blazak has observed street families and the powerful psychological effect they can have on their followers. "Take the kids out of this situation and they'll say it was wrong, what was I doing? It's the same as sports riots. You talk to someone and say, 'How come yesterday you were over-turning cars?' And they will say they got caught up in it."

Some of the teenagers in the Thantos Family,[1] especially the minor members like Sarah Caster and Crystal Ivey, were relatively normal teenagers going through a rocky time. If they had not encountered the street family culture, they would probably have had survived adolescence and arrived at adulthood intact. Instead, they were sucked into a world that dismantled their morals and principles, forever altering their futures and the future of the Williams family [adoptive family of the victim, Jessica Kate Williams].

Others in the family were fundamentally disturbed, including Carl Alsup and Cassandra Hale. In the street family society, they found a home that nourished their malignancies and extinguished any hope they had of intervention. Shelter staff reinforced their fantasy identities by calling them by their

1. The Thantos Family was a group of street kids in Portland, Oregon, who murdered a mentally challenged woman.

made-up names. On the streets, their crimes went ignored by the media and the outside world. And so, they thought they could get away with anything.

Still others were damaged and vulnerable, such as Jimmy Stewart. Their vulnerabilities were exploited by the more cunning and violent in the street family society. For a genuinely homeless youth, the street family offers a powerful lure of protection and guidance. And one youth, Danielle Cox, remains an enigma, a child of middle-class privilege driven by motivations perhaps even she could not fathom. Together, these young people descended into group violence if for no other reason than that they could, and no one stopped them.

Regardless of their backgrounds, most of the street kids in the Thantos Family seemed disconnected from themselves and representative of a society where young adults are encouraged to immerse themselves in fantasy games. The result is young people who are allowed to divorce themselves fully from reality and pretend to be magical characters. For teenagers still developing a sense of moral obligation and ethics, these fantasy identities play a frightening trick: no longer themselves, they are severed from their consciences and the consequences of their actions. Everything becomes a mirage: it is all only kidding, only pretend, and even when someone is brutally murdered, the drama only continues in new and exciting forms.

Periodical and Internet Sources Bibliography

The following articles have been selected to supplement the diverse views presented in this chapter.

Nancy Cambria	"Teens Can Find Haven in Unlikely Place," *St. Louis Today*, November 1, 2010. www.stltoday.com.
Jim Diers	"From the Ground Up: Community's Role in Addressing Street-Level Social Issues," *Social Policy*, Spring 2010, pp. 23–34.
Tom Gallagher	"A Pathway to Hope for Homeless Teens," *National Catholic Reporter*, vol. 47, no. 1, October 29, 2010, p. 19.
Larry Miller	"The Hidden Homeless: Teenagers," *Philadelphia Tribune*, July 28, 2010. Newamericanmedia.org.
Von E. Nebbitt, Laura E. House, Sanna J. Thompson, David E. Pollio	"Successful Transitions of Runaway/Homeless Youth from Shelter Care," *Journal of Child & Family Studies*, vol. 16, 2007, pp. 545–55.
Camilla Pemberton	"No Room at the Refuge," *Community Care*, vol. 211, May 6, 2010.
Lenard D. Prewitt	"Helping Youths on the Streets," *Behavioral Healthcare*, vol. 26, no. 5, May 2006, pp. 46–47.
Rick Toma	"A Critical Look at the Foster Care System: Foster Care Outcomes," *Lifting the Veil*, May 16, 2010. www.liftingtheveil.org.

Are Street Teens
a Global Problem?

Chapter Preface

Mario R. Capecchi was born in Verona, Italy, on October 6, 1937, to a poet and an Italian air force officer who chose not to marry. When he was three years old, his mother was imprisoned by the Nazis. Anticipating her arrest, she had given money to a peasant family to take in her son. As he relates:

> For reasons that have never been clear to me, my mother's money ran out after one year and, at age 4½, I set off on my own. I headed south, sometimes living in the streets, sometimes joining gangs of other homeless children, sometimes living in orphanages, and most of the time being hungry. My recollections of those four years are vivid but not continuous, rather like a series of snapshots. Some of them are brutal beyond description, others more palatable.

Capecchi was reunited with his mother when he was nine years old, had his first bath in six years, and began the process of learning how to read and write. In November 2007, he was awarded the Nobel Prize in medicine for his work in genetics. In relating his early experiences on the street to his success, Capecchi said in an interview immediately following the announcement of his award, "I think what it provided was resourcefulness, and I think just the drive to keep yourself, maintain yourself, and survive. I think it led me to be able to use my own resources, to be able to get through life. . . . Most children didn't make it. I think I was extremely lucky."

> My name is Ricardo and I am 16. . . . I've been living on the street for the last six years. . . . In the morning I wake up and wash my face—in the fountain if I sleep in the plaza or outside the cinema and in the sea if I sleep in the bathroom. Then I work til 4PM. . . . My dreams for the future are that I

could work in a bakery, live in a proper concrete house, have a wife and start my own family. . . . But in reality none of this will happen to me.

This is the story of Ricardo, a street teen from Montevideo, Uruguay, as told to a writer for the *New Internationalist*. It is a stark contrast to the success story of Mario R. Capecchi, a street child of another era. Unfortunately, Ricardo's story of deprivation and despair is all too common worldwide. Although it is difficult to make an accurate count of street children, such sources as Amnesty International and UNICEF estimate there are between 150 and 100 million worldwide. Their lot is a grim one. Many of these children resort to petty theft and prostitution to survive. They are at risk of contracting diseases, especially sexually transmitted diseases. And many are addicted to drugs, alcohol, or inhalants. With no education and no support system, the future for these children is bleak. Disease, war, and natural disasters have dramatically increased the number of street children worldwide in recent years. Increased numbers of children are losing their parents to diseases such as AIDS, to natural disasters such as the Haiti earthquake and South Asian tsunami of 2004, and to ethnic cleansing and genocide in such countries as Rwanda and Bosnia. With no one to turn to, these children turn to the streets to fight for survival. The global impact of street children is debated in the viewpoints in the following chapter.

> *"Instead of aid and protection from the adult world . . . these children can anticipate only hostility—or much worse—from the grown-up world."*

Street Youth Are Vulnerable and Need to Be Saved

Kevin Clarke

There are more than 150 million street children worldwide and few countries are doing anything to help them, maintains the author in the following viewpoint. In extreme cases, some countries have executed street children in an attempt to clean up their streets. In other cases, such as in Mexico City, children are being removed from the street, but it remains unclear if these children will be given homes. Kevin Clarke is a senior editor at U.S. Catholic *and the online content manager for Claretian Publications.*

As you read, consider the following questions:

1. What are some of the reasons children end up on the streets, according to the author?

2. What countries does Human Rights Watch say have been responsible for executing street children, as cited by the author?

3. What does the author say is the goal of the UN's Millennium Challenge?

If you have ever visited Mexico City you may have enjoyed their antics as part of the federal district's colorful backdrop. Maybe you can spot them edging out from the corner of your vacation photos: the late-night Chiclets salesmen, the street jugglers and clowns, the grinning, cajoling panhandlers.

Mexico City Now Bans Street Children

They are Mexico City's street children, tolerated, even subtly promoted as part of the city's charm.

Their day lives entertaining or huckstering on the streets certainly seem charming enough. It's the night lives of these often abandoned and forgotten kids that can get a little less pleasantly cinematic. Stalked by hunger and filth and the worst kind of adult predators, huffing gasoline or paint to dull the pain of their so-called childhoods and stiff-arm the hunger that pursues them, these kids are living more Mad Max than Tom Sawyer.

For the kids of Mexico City, at least, their days on the streets may be numbered. There has been growing pressure from federal authorities to do something—finally—about the nation's street children. A new law proposes a "ban" on street children, requiring municipal officials to find a safe refuge via social service agencies for these children or face fines of $420 per child left unattended. It's a dramatic proposal aimed at resolving one of the developing world's most persistent and troubling social phenomena.

Wilfred Hildonen/Cartoonstock.

There Are 150 Million Street Children Worldwide

Depending on how they are defined—some kids maintain loose connections to parents and families in households, some have been completely abandoned to the streets—the world is crowded with as many as 150 million street children. Fleeing abusive parents or institutions, orphaned by drugs, poverty, war, or AIDS, the children endure a feral, desperate, and sometimes short existence. In Latin America, Asia, and Africa, the plight of street children has festered in plain sight for decades. In the United States an estimated 1.3 million kids live on our cities' streets.

Instead of aid and protection from the adult world that swirls around them, these children can anticipate only hostility—or much worse—from the grown-up world because of the kinds of things they do to survive. The begging and thievery that is their daily bread and butter make them constant petty irritants to local shopkeepers and police—"society's garbage," as one police officer in the Philippines said.

In some countries there is clear evidence that police vigilante squads have taken to cleaning up their municipal streets by liquidating the source of the problem, these unprotected children. The summary execution of children in Guatemala, Brazil, the Philippines, and other nations has been documented by Human Rights Watch.

Mexican authorities say they are now ready to respond to the plight of these abandoned children, but it's unclear if their solution represents a sincere commitment to rebuilding childhoods or a familiar effort to simply, sometimes ruthlessly, remove the problem from view.

These Children Can Be Saved

The saddest aspect of the deplorable state of these children is that it does not have to be this way. It would not take much to respond appropriately to the aching need of the world's abandoned children, not with the authoritative municipal sweep they've already experienced, but with the parental embrace they deserve.

That has been part of the promise of the UN's Millennium Challenge Project to cut world poverty in half by 2015, a commitment the United States has joined along with every industrial power on earth. We are already falling far behind on those goals, however.

A fraction of what the world's assembly of nations almost casually commits to arms production would be enough to save every one of these kids, to offer them clothing and cleanliness, safety and shelter, adequate nutrition.

We freely do as much for our own children. Can we find the political will to recover these childhoods lost, to accept these children as our own, and save them once and for all from the streets?

> "We paint a picture of young people who
> negotiate resilient trajectories, strength-
> ened in part by personal resources
> (albeit unconventional), bonds to their
> peer groups, and religiosity."

Many Street Teens Are Resilient and Adapt Well to Street Life

Macalane J. Malindi and Linda C. Theron

Contrary to traditional thinking that categorizes street children as vulnerable, they are actually quite resilient, contend the authors in the following viewpoint. In a study of twenty street children from South Africa, the authors found their subjects to be street savvy and to have considerable inner strength. These children gain their resilience from conventional practices, such as knowing where to find shelter, and unconventional practices, including forming personal bonds through teasing each other. Macalane J. Malindi and Linda C. Theron are affiliated with the school of education sciences, North-West University, Vanderbijl-park, South Africa.

Macalane J. Malindi and Linda C. Theron, "The Hidden Resilience of Street Youth," *South African Journal of Psychology*, vol. 40, no. 3, 2010, pp. 318–26.

As you read, consider the following questions:

1. According to the authors, what are some of the qualities traditionally ascribed to street children?

2. What are some of the dangers that children are exposed to on the street, according to the authors?

3. What are some of the unconventional practices of street children that promote resilience, according to the authors?

Street children exhibit powerful signs of resilience, albeit hidden. 'Hidden resilience' is a relatively novel concept, which refers to patterns of living that may not always fit in with mainstream psychological theories, or community conceptualization, of socially appropriate behaviour, but that nevertheless encourage youth to bounce back from hardship. Traditionally, street children are not viewed as resilient. Rather, they are conceptualised as vulnerable, deviant, and maladaptive youth who suffer from a range of psychological disorders. Their patterns of living and risk are seen as almost synonymous: in addition to the complex social and familial risks that compel street children to choose life on the streets, on the street, they are vulnerable to all sorts of additional risks such as reckless motorists, inadequate shelter, abusive police officers, drugs, crime, prostitution syndicates, and bigger/older street youth who taunt and intimidate them. More recently, some emerging literature has begun to challenge the notion of street children as helpless and hapless beings. . . .

Street Youth Gain Strength in Unconventional Ways

Resilience was central to the stories told by the street youth [twenty South African youths] in this study. As such, the findings add to nascent descriptions of street youth as hardy. Moreover, the findings boost the relatively novel understanding of hidden resilience—clearly street youth bounce back because they are not afraid to navigate unconventional paths.

Although participants reported many instances of normative resilience-promoting mechanisms (such as asking for help, being assertive, reciprocating support, and making the most of shelters), their resilience was also informed by unconventional practices (including teasing one another in an attempt to provide humorous relief, engaging in violence, vandalising public property, telling lies, bonding with other street youth) and by values not typically associated with street youth (such as religiosity and purposeful regulation of behaviour). As with other cohorts of youth whose resilience are typically overlooked, participants combined pro-social practices and unconventional mechanisms to rebound. While behaviours such as vandalising public property or stabbing an assailant cannot be condoned, they emphasise that street youth possess agency and assertiveness that can be channelled. Stories of street youth adjusting their public behaviour suggest a streetwise savvy, ingenuity, and flexibility. They also contradict perceptions of street youth as unmindful of the norms of society. In other words, embedded in the unconventional practices recounted by our participants are the seeds of resilience. Rather than judge or stereotype street youth, theorists and practitioners need to acknowledge that these coping mechanisms contain embryonic antecedents of resilience and nurture them.

It is not expected that street children are religious. Their religiosity is obscured by prejudice, as is the rich resilience-promoting value of street youths' peer group. The finding that participants' resilience was rooted in religion and peer-group belonging warns against traditional stereotypes of street children and their peer groups as deviant and maladaptive. These findings challenge service providers and mental health practitioners to recognise and build on resilience-promoting values and practices of street youth.

Street Children in Peru Demonstrate Resilience

There are many street children in Peru. And a large number of them, mainly boys, . . . had been living on the streets of Lima. Most of them, ages 14 years of age and under, were using one or more drugs nearly every day. . . .

The amazing thing was the resilience many of these street children demonstrated.

Edith Henderson Grotberg,
"Resilience in Street Children and in Victims of
Political Violence in Peru," Resilience Net, 2006.

Street Youth Deserve Respect

All of the above cautions against a charity approach of rescuing street children. It also militates against the age-old deficit perspective of street children as perennially vulnerable. Instead, the findings urge recognition of street youth's strengths and of the embryonic forms of their resilience and an asset-based approach to interventions with street youth. The transformed perspective of street youth as resilient young people implies that they should be co-authors of any interventions aimed at enabling them further. . . .

Our findings transform the popular, medically inclined conceptualisation of street youth as perennially helpless, vulnerable and maladapted. In its place, we paint a picture of young people who negotiate resilient trajectories, strengthened in part by personal resources (albeit unconventional), bonds to their peer groups, and religiosity. This strength-based approach is in line with positive psychology, which focuses on unearthing strengths or assets that maintain wellbeing rather than on weaknesses that negate wellness. This does not mean that we whitewash the many challenges street youth face or condone antisocial coping mechanisms. Instead, we urge celebration of their rich ability to bounce back. In a country such as South Africa with its legacy of negative stereotypes and fundamental disrespect for fellow human beings, it is high time that we extend respect to street youth as well and celebrate their resilience while amplifying its antecedents.

> *"Many believe the most serious threat to street children comes from the very people responsible for their safety and protection—local governmental and law enforcement officials."*

Street Children Are Often Victims of Police Brutality

Evgenia Berezina

Too often, police regard street children as victimizers, rather than perceiving them as the victims they are, according to Evgenia Berezina in the following viewpoint. With this mindset, police feel justified in brutalizing these children in the attempts by law enforcement to clean the streets and solve petty crimes, states the author. Sadly, the attitude of the police reflects the attitude of society at large—mainly indifference to the problems of these vulnerable children—the author claims. Evgenia Berezina is senior executive assistant at the Youth Advocate Program International. She is also a Fulbright fellow on violence and discrimination issues.

Evgenia Berezina, "Victimization and Abuse of Street Children Worldwide," *Youth Advocate Program International Resource Paper*, December 2004. www.yapi.org. Copyright © 2004 by Youth Advocate Program International, Inc. All rights reserved. Reproduced by permission.

As you read, consider the following questions:

1. What is the mortality rate of street children, according to the author?

2. What are some of the diseases that street children are subject to, according to the author?

3. Why are street children easy targets of police and security forces, according to the author?

They are dirty, scared, bitter, worn out and helpless; these little street survivors grow up much too soon and die much too young. They upset our consciousness and disrupt the comforting illusion of public well-being. They are children. And, they are assaulted, tortured, and killed everyday.

Most Street Children Are Victims of Abuse

According to recent UN data, there are nearly 150 million street children in the world today, and the number is rising daily. That means nearly one of every 60 people living on the planet is a child living on the streets. Half of them die within first four years of their street life. In other words, a child who ends up in the street at age 8 has a 50% chance of dying before the age of 12.

There are many unfortunate incidents which cause children as young as 3 years old to end up on the streets. The vast majority of these children have been abused and abandoned by their own families. In Guatemala, for instance, 64% of street girls interviewed by *Human Rights Watch* turned out to be victims of incest. Other reasons include extreme poverty of a family, death of parents, unstable socio-economic situation in the country, and armed conflicts that cause many people to flee their homes, therefore instigating many families to fall apart.

Once on the street, children must resort to begging, robbery, and even prostitution in order to survive. Many join gangs where they are introduced to crime, violence, and drugs. They become addicted to inhaling glue, paint thinner, and/or other toxic substances destroying brain cells and organ tissues. Street educators in Guatemala, Mexico, Honduras, Russia, and other countries regularly find numerous grossly intoxicated kids as young as 6 years old trying to escape the pain, hunger, and desolation of street life in the poisonous fumes.

Street Children Are Exploited

Neglected by society and government, street children are deprived of education, proper nutrition, and medical care. They suffer and die from various, often easily treatable, diseases such as head lice, skin parasites, pneumonia, tuberculosis and a host of sexually transmitted diseases, including, yet not limited to, gonorrhea, syphilis and AIDS. Because of the grave lack of outreach and shelter programs, street children often have no place to go and no one from whom they can seek help and protection.

Protection is what these street children desperately need because they are prime targets of disturbed, exploitive adults. Child murderers, angry shopkeepers, and pedophiles are a daily threat to the safety and lives of desperate street children. . . .

Police Brutality Is Common

Many believe the most serious threat to street children comes from the very people responsible for their safety and protection—local governmental and law enforcement officials. Unfortunately, police brutality and corruption is common worldwide, and is especially widespread in developing countries with large populations of street children. Unspeakable police brutality reflects the governments' perception of street children as parasites to be exterminated, rather than as children needing homes and nurturing. A growing number of politicians inaccurately blame increasing levels of violent crime on children and teens, instead of looking at the actual numbers of street children who are victimized or murdered on a regular basis by official security forces.

Police overwhelmingly view and treat these street children as sub-human; unworthy of basic human rights. While it is true that street children are sometimes involved in petty theft, drug-trafficking, and other criminal activities, the police often assume that violence and brutality are the only means of dealing with this problem. They unjustifiably see a hardened criminal in every street child. For the police and other security forces, street children represent easy and silent targets. They are young, small, poor, ignorant of their rights, and often have no family or advocates who will come to their defense. It does not require much time or effort to detain and torture a child to coerce a confession, and street children are unlikely to register formal complaints.

Latin American countries are especially notorious for their vicious and sadistic practices against street children. Death squads and armed police forces regularly comb the city streets to perform savage "social cleansings". In Honduras, brutal murders of street kids by government forces reached such high levels that it led to an international scandal in 2001. The UN appointed a Special Rapporteur to investigate hundreds of extrajudicial executions of street children throughout the country. Numerous witnesses saw armed men in civilian clothes that drove around in unmarked vehicles and had, on several occasions, forcibly abducted street children. Often their dead bodies were found in deserted areas outside the city limits. The children appear to have been tortured before being shot in the head, execution-style. Police, meanwhile, demonstrated an alarming lack of concern with the situation, and, at times actively covered up the crimes, including failing to record and investigate the murders, and quietly disposing of evidence.

A Brazilian Child Tells of Police Brutality

Many policemen there, you're not doing anything, they book you, they beat you, they humiliate you. They humiliate you, they call you a thief in front of everyone ... they throw you to the ground ... they take you ... (he sighed) they take you to the rear ... they take you to the darkness, they beat you, they give you black eyes, they leave you beaten up, with legs and back full of marks. And I wouldn't wish this on anyone. Have marks on the hand, the body, the face. The worst place to be beaten is the face. The worst place they always choose is the face. If they don't go for the face they shoot at us. We can be at that distance, they give us electric shocks.

M.O. Ribeiro,
"Street Children and Their Relationship with the Police,"
International Nursing Review, *March 2008.*

Police actions are informally sanctioned by high ranking governmental officials. For example, the Minister for Public Security of Honduras denied any police involvement in the killing of any street child. The children, according to him, were "out of their minds" and not to be trusted. His point of view was fully supported by the country's Human Rights Commissioner, whose son [Rodrigo Valladares Pineda] incidentally, was arrested in November 2000 for attacking a 10 year old street boy and poking a lit cigarette in his eye.

Street Children Are Often Arbitrarily Detained

Arbitrary detention of street children is also a common practice, even though it grossly violates international and domestic laws. Law enforcement and government authorities often try to justify roundups or prolonged detention of street children as means of identifying them and re-uniting them with their families. Neither the manner of the arrests or the lack of actual re-unification attempts reflects this law enforcement "justification". In fact, many street children often have no family to claim them. Meanwhile, they are held in deplorable conditions. In some instances, the police beat detained street children claiming that it is a method of crime prevention. In Bulgaria, for example, children who have been held in lock-ups reported that they were beaten by police with electric shock batons, clubs, chains, rubber hosing, boxing gloves, and a metal rod with a ball at the end. In Paraguay, police practiced interrogation of street children by placing plastic bags over their heads while they proceeded to kick and hit their bodies, especially the testicles and the back. Police are known to place pins under the children's fingernails and give them electric shocks. The hypocrisy of the authorities is most evident if one considers that the police are especially active in "cleaning up" the streets at times of major events that attract close national and international attention. The children are arrested on vague or false charges, sometimes just for being homeless or for begging. Brute force and obscene language are used in abundance by police during roundups that frequently happen at night, in order to avoid public witnesses and political condemnation. Many street children have described being grabbed, kicked, hit, whipped, caned, and/or clubbed while being held in police custody.

Street Children Are Extorted

Security forces have also been known to abuse and exploit street children for personal gain. One commonly reported practice is for the police to extort money or services from the children by threatening to imprison them if they refuse to pay. A Kenyan street boy shared his experience with *Human Rights*

Watch: "We usually carry sacks (for garbage picking). The police beat us up and put us in our sacks. Even if we're just walking around, doing nothing. If you don't give them money, they take you to the station. . . They search us. If we have money, they take it." A Guatemalan street child said, ". . .they take you down to the station and make you clean it—they say they'll arrest you if you don't. On the street and also at the station; they'll hit us in front of the other police. Also they step on our hands with the heels of their boots and press down hard and twist."

Girls living on the streets are especially vulnerable to sexual abuse from security forces that sometimes coerce street girls into sexual acts in exchange for their freedom. In extreme cases, police will blatantly rape girls and threaten to kill or maim them if they report the abuse.

From police custody, the children may be sent before a juvenile court which often places them in special institutions called "remands", or juvenile homes. The remands are mostly degenerated into jail-like custodial centers. Many children sent to such homes in India and Latin America have died as a result of severe beatings and torture performed either by the staff or by older children.

Few advocates, lawyers, or prosecutors speak up for these abused children who rarely have the financial resources to pay legal fees. Family members willing to intervene usually have financial constraints of their own. The street children's stories remain untold, and their lives are often neglected and forgotten.

Widespread impunity allows violence against street children to continue. Casa Alianza in Latin America files hundreds of criminal complaints on behalf of street children each year, but only a handful result in prosecution. Almost always when an investigation is ordered, it is done by the police themselves, and in some cases, by members of the same department, station, or remand house staff in which the alleged abuse occurred.

Society Neglects Street Children

Adding to the police brutality is the cruelty and indifference of society as a whole, which has turned its eyes and hearts away from the children of the street. . . . In Guatemala, street children are often murdered when they fall asleep in public places. Casa Alianza's reports that a homeless boy was killed by three unidentified civilians who covered the boy's head with a cloth as he slept then crushed his skull with a concrete block. The shocking ruthlessness of the murders and abuse, and the fact that there has been so little public outcry, seems to illustrate the general disregard for street children by the public.

Street children desperately need programs and services. Unfortunately, there are relatively few shelters or outreach programs anywhere in the world. And the ones that do exist, like at Casa Alianza, struggle daily for justice and the recognition of the human rights of street children. Governments need stronger enforcement measures and international penalties for non-compliance. Police must be made accountable for their crimes against homeless and poor children. There is much to be done.

"For the past two decades, the 13 million residents of Nigeria's biggest city have run the gauntlet of several thousand delinquent youths who roam the street extorting money."

Street Youth Are a Menace to Society in Nigeria

Toye Olori

People in Lagos, Nigeria, are harassed on a daily basis by several thousand street children who extort money from them, according to Toye Olori. Called Area Boys, these youth have resisted past attempts to rehabilitate them and remain on the streets, threatening citizens, demanding money, committing crimes, and sometimes resorting to violence. Toye Olori wrote the following viewpoint for News from Africa, *an independent online news agency that publishes news and feature stories written from an African perspective.*

As you read, consider the following questions:

1. Where does the article claim the Area Boys hang out in Lagos, and whom do they harass for money?

2. What does the UN Office on Drugs and Crime blame for the emergence of these gangs, according to the article?

3. What program has the governor of Lagos state set up to attempt to rehabilitate Area Boys, as stated in the article?

After buying a new television in a popular market in Nigeria's commercial capital Lagos, Ade Ojelabi was wending his way home when four unkempt young men suddenly surrounded his taxi.

"You will have to pay money for the ground," growled one of the youths, with bloodshot eyes, leaning at the window where Ojelabi sat.

"Otherwise I will stab you in the eye," barked another with yellowing teeth from the opposite side of the car, as he brandished a large screwdriver.

With the car stuck fast in traffic that clogs Lagos' streets on a daily basis, a speedy escape was not an option.

As passers-by watched from a safe distance, fearful of intervening, the taxi driver advised Ojelabi that he would have to part with some cash.

His initial offer of 200 naira (US $1.5) was rejected. But when he increased it to 500 naira (US $3.7), the youths grabbed the banknotes and went on their way.

"More blessings to you!" they said, smiling as they scarpered off. "May your son never be like us," one of them added.

The Area Boys Bully People for Money

Ojelabi's ordeal is one played out every day on the streets of Lagos. For the past two decades, the 13 million residents of Nigeria's biggest city have run the gauntlet of several thousand delinquent youths who roam the streets extorting money.

Known as Area Boys—although a few are female—they sprang up in the early 1980s. To begin with they were just small bands of bullies who roamed the slums adjoining the central business district. But since then their numbers have burgeoned, fed by the steady flood of unemployed people that migrates constantly into Lagos from elsewhere in the country.

The Area Boys are now rampant all over the city. Their favourite hangouts are bus stops, major highways and markets. In broad daylight, they levy tolls on bus drivers, they demand bribes from market women wanting to set up stalls for the day, they patrol potential car-parking spaces and demand illegal fees from shoppers. They even threaten ordinary passerbys, demanding "donations".

A study by the Nigerian branch of the UN Office on Drugs and Crime blamed their emergence on the "complex dynamics of socio-economic deprivation" that confronts young people in cities.

While other Nigerian cities have their own hoodlums, there is nothing as brazen or ubiquitous as the Area Boys of Lagos. "The coercive and persuasive requests, petty crimes and sometimes-violent offences by the Area Boys to acquire resources, generally cash in the urban main business and crowded areas, has disturbed the civil society and defied the civic authority," the 2002 UN report said.

Wale Adenaike, a self-confessed Area Boy, said how he had dropped out of secondary school at 16 after his father could no longer pay his fees. Swapping the classroom for the streets, the youngster quickly became addicted to drugs.

Now aged 25, he makes his living by claiming ownership of a space by a road junction in the central business district of Lagos and charging motorists to leave their cars there. "Otherwise, I make a living out of trouble," he said nonchalantly. Adenaike went on to explain that he and his friends were also available to be hired as thugs and for "other odd jobs".

This is something that worries the authorities who see the Area Boys as a pool of troublemakers ready to be recruited for the bouts of ethnic, religious and political violence that intermittently erupt in Lagos.

Attempts Have Been Made to Rehabilitate the Area Boys

Past governments have made various attempts to get the Area Boys off the streets and rehabilitate them by teaching them artisan skills and trades. General Ibrahim Babangida, Nigeria's military ruler from 1985 to 1993, established a People's Bank, which extended micro-credits to many street boys and girls to help them start small businesses. However, there was not enough money to go round. And many of those who benefited from the handouts simply returned to the streets when People's Bank collapsed in the late 1990s.

Now Bola Tinubu, the governor of Lagos State since the return of democracy in 1999, has designed a new scheme to rid the city of the Area Boy scourge. He has set up a skills training centre at Ita Oko, a disused island prison in Lagos lagoon, to the east of the city. Area Boys will be taken there for six months of training, and will receive a certificate and a job placement at the end of it.

"We cannot continue to give them fish. We have decided to teach them how to catch fish," Tinubu said during a recent visit to the training centre. But he added sternly that all those who reject the offer of rehabilitation "must be ready to leave Lagos".

Adenaike, the self-proclaimed Area Boy, said he would relish the chance to get on a rehabilitation programme that would help wean him off drugs, teach him some skills and give him the chance of a new life. The scheme is due to be launched soon, but until then Adenaike must wait. So too must the citizens of Lagos who continue to suffer daily harassment.

In May, a group of Area Boys attacked and stabbed a soldier in the Oshodi district of Lagos after he challenged them for trying to extort money from a bus driver. This attack prompted a series of reprisal raids by troops in different parts of the city over a two-week period. According to reports by eyewitnesses and local newspapers, dozens of Area Boys were killed in the crackdown. And more than 200 street boys arrested by the soldiers were handed over to the police.

A Police Crackdown Was Controversial

For several weeks afterwards the Area Boys were noticeably absent from the streets. Market women and bus drivers staged public rallies in support of the soldiers. Riding on the crest of a wave of apparent public approval, the police launched further raids and made more arrests. "We can't allow the Area Boys to continue being a nuisance to the public and harassing innocent citizens," Ade Ajakaiye, the city's police commissioner, told reporters in June.

Human rights activists are not only worried about the soldiers' heavy-handed tactics. They are also convinced that the recent crackdown by the security forces will only provide a temporary respite. Already the local media is reporting a gradual return of the Area Boys to their streets, where they are resuming their old habits.

"From our perspective the military intervention did not follow due process," said Joseph Amenaghawon of Social and Economic Rights Action (SERAC), a local non-governmental organisation. "When soldiers feel threatened by the actions of civilians, they should not take the law into their hands but should lodge complaints with the police," he said.

Amenaghawon blamed the activities of the Area Boys on decades of misrule by a succession of military and civilian governments. Although Nigeria is the largest oil producer in Africa, more than two-thirds of its estimated 126 million people live below the poverty line.

"Area Boys are part of the offshoots of underlying problems," said Amenaghawon. "If there is a real policy for dealing with youth unemployment, Area Boys will fizzle out over time. If not they will only multiply."

"Once children become detached from
their families, they are harder to reach
as they drop out of school and, therefore, out of the reach of school nurses."

Community Nurses Can Help
UK Street Teens

Alison Moore

*Community and school nurses can play an important role in
identifying children at risk of becoming runaways and intervene
at a stage early enough to help them deal with their problems
constructively, claims Alison Moore in the following viewpoint.
Many of these at-risk children come from homes where parents
abuse drugs or have mental problems, and some children have
been sexually abused. These are often families who aren't using
social services, so a school nurse might be in the best position to
identify troubled children, Moore suggests. Alison Moore is a
journalist who has written for the* Nursing Standard *from which
this viewpoint is taken.*

As you read, consider the following questions:

1. What is the typical age of runaway children in the UK,
   according to the author?

Alison Moore, "Runaways at Risk," *Nursing Standard*, vol. 24, no. 32, April 14, 2010,
pp. 18–19. Original article submission by author. All rights reserved. Reproduced by
permission of Alison Moore.

2. How many UK children run away from home for more than four weeks, according to the author?

3. With so few "safe beds" available to UK runaways, where do they often end up sleeping, according to the author?

Children who run away are at risk in many ways, from drug and alcohol addiction and mental health problems, to sexually transmitted infections and pregnancy associated with sexual exploitation or rape.

Runaway children tend to be aged around 13 or 14, but 10 percent will be below ten. Two thirds will not be reported missing to the police. Up to 10,000 will be away from home for more than four weeks.

Yet children who run away are almost invisible to the NHS [National Health Service] and other agencies. They tend to avoid contact with the 'authorities' fearing they will be sent home. Services are not targeted at them when they are at risk of running away, when they are away from home or when they return.

Little Awareness

Children's Society policy adviser Susie Ramsay says that the public has little awareness of this issue.

The Queen's Nursing Institute's homeless health initiative manager, Kate Tansley, says: 'Health care to support these children is variable. They will not necessarily be registered with a GP [general practitioner] and may only turn up in places such as A&E [hospital emergency departments]. Young runaways may not be seen as homeless. This can be a problem if their needs are not identified. They could have complex needs requiring follow-up.'

Some areas have identified runaway children—whether they are living rough or 'sofa surfing' with friends or relatives—as a priority and are developing multi-agency services

---

Life for Young UK Runaways

Research involving 103 young people found:

- All had misused drugs or alcohol.
- Only a quarter had received early intervention to sort out problems in their lives.
- Some had experienced barriers to accessing support, such as not knowing where to go. Most did not seek help.
- Half had experienced physical abuse while at home. A small number had been sexually abused.
- Many came from chaotic households, with substance misuse, domestic violence and mental health problems. Fathers were often absent.

TAKEN FROM: Alison Moore, "Runaways at Risk," *Nursing Standard*, vol. 24, no. 32, April 14, 2010.

---

to support them. But only around one in ten councils have any form of runaway project, says Ms Ramsay.

In parts of Lancashire, runaway children may be offered sexual health, drug and alcohol services, as well as other health services. They are offered support to return home, where work with the family may follow.

Pauline Geraghty, programme manager of the Lancashire Streetsafe project, which is run by the Children's Society, says offering runaways somewhere to stay is a problem.

'There is no independent safe place in which to put young people,' she says. 'People have to make some really difficult decisions. Do they return the child to the family or not?'

Safe Houses

Railway Children deals with homeless children in the UK and abroad. The charity is calling for a network of emergency safe houses for children exposed to violence, drug misuse, sexual exploitation and other crime while on the streets.

There are only nine 'safe refuge' beds available in England, so children have to sleep in police stations or strangers' homes.

The recent announcement that the London Refuge, run by St Christopher's Fellowship, is going to close because of a funding shortfall will reduce the number of beds even further.

Early Intervention

Health professionals are urged to take action. Railway Children's national strategy and policy officer Andy McCullough highlights the need for early intervention to reach those at risk of becoming 'detached'.

Many children who end up living on the streets come from families where the adults take drugs, have mental health problems or experience some form of domestic violence.

Sexual abuse by a family member may be the cause of a child running away. Others may be gay and encounter family hostility. A disproportionate number come from social housing, while others run away from care.

Mr McCullough says these are often the families who cannot be reached through the existing services. They will not use children's centres or youth clubs.

But community-based nurses and school nurses might be able to identify children at risk, and intervene. Some children may benefit from child and adolescent mental health services.

Early intervention is key. Once children become detached from their families, they are harder to reach as they drop out of school and, therefore, out of the reach of school nurses.

Health Services

While they are away from home, these children are unlikely to access health services. However, in a crisis they may attend A&E.

Mr McCullough urges A&E departments to provide information about local services for young people and ensure staff have telephone numbers to give out.

Children who go missing and then return home are supposed to be interviewed by the police. In some areas, they will have an independent interview with an organisation such as the Children's Society. These may help to tease out the reason for running away and reveal any harm the child may have come to.

Because many young people will not be reported missing, they will not receive this help. Therefore it is important that other health services reach out to them. 'They will need to engage with them on the streets and in the squats and soup kitchens,' says Mr McCullough.

'For health service staff, that might mean working with less information than they would normally have, and developing trust with the young people.'

Healthcare workers may want to call the police or social services, especially if they feel the child is at risk. But Mr McCullough points out that children are likely to leave the hospital or healthcare setting if social services are involved.

Confidentiality Issues

'There are many issues around confidentiality,' he says. 'Healthcare professionals may need to work with a young person for some time before they find out what is going on in his or her life. Trust comes up again and again. Young people test you to see how you respond to certain bits of information.'

But there can be a fine line when deciding how much to intervene. Mr McCullough has worked with homeless young people for more than 20 years, and as a father himself knows parenting decisions are often difficult. He says he frequently wonders 'whether that young person I saw today will turn up tomorrow'.

Periodical and Internet Sources Bibliography

The following articles have been selected to supplement the diverse views presented in this chapter.

Hamid Reza Ahmadkhaniha, Seyed Vahid Shariat, Sharif Torkaman-nejad, and Mohammad Mehdi Hoseini Moghadam	"The Frequency of Sexual Abuse and Depression in a Sample of Street Children of One of the Deprived Districts of Tehran," *Journal of Child Sexual Abuse*, vol. 16, no. 4, 2007, pp. 23–35.
Alessandro Conticini and David Hulme	"Escaping Violence, Seeking Freedom: Why Children in Bangladesh Migrate to the Street," *Development and Change*, vol. 38, 2007, pp. 201–27.
Sterling Herron	"The Street Children of Peru," *HCCHS Student News*, November 8, 2010. Yourstudentnews.com.
Muhammad Waheed Iqbal	"Street Children: An Overlooked Issue in Pakistan," *Child Abuse Review*, vol. 17, no. 3, 2008, pp. 201–09.
Akua Kjanie	"A Continent of Beggars?" *Natna*, April 27, 2010. Natna.wordpress.com.
David McKenzie	"Kenya's Street Teens Struggle to Survive," CNN.com, November 6, 2009, Edition.cnn.com.
Stefan Savenstedt and Terttu Häggstrom	"Working with Girls Living on the Streets in East Africa: Professionals' Experiences," *Journal of Advanced Nursing*, vol. 50, no. 5, June 2005, pp. 489–97.
Noam Schimmel	"Freedom and Autonomy of Street Children," *International Journal of Children's Rights*, vol. 14, 2006, pp. 211–33.

For Further Discussion

Chapter 1

1. Ruby J. Martinez cites a study that found most teens run away from home to gain control over their lives. Noam Schimmel argues that youth lose control of their lives on the streets. Are these arguments mutually exclusive? In what ways do street teens take control of their lives by running away from a bad situation at home? In what ways do they lose control of their lives on the street?

2. Ian Urbina writes that the economic recession has increased the number of runaway teens. What impact do you think a recession has on family life that could create a situation that a teen wants to run from? What are some of the reasons children might be abandoned by their family during a recession?

Chapter 2

1. Viewpoints by Maureen Blaha and by M. Rosa Solorio and others cite research showing that a significant number of street teens are victims of commercial sexual exploitation and risky sexual behavior. What are some of the results of this victimization and behavior?

Chapter 3

1. Two differing perspectives on foster care are provided in Chapter 3. Meghan Stromberg writes that for younger children, placement in a foster home is often the best option for those living on the street. Carol Smith writes about the failures of the foster care system, citing the number of older teens who end up on the streets after

"aging out" of the foster care system. What are some of the reasons each writer gives for her differing perspective? What solutions do they see?

2. The phenomenon of street families is explored in viewpoints written by Joanne O'Sullivan Oliveira, Pamela J. Burke, and Rene Denfeld. The first two write that street families can help makes street teens safer, while Denfeld finds that street teens can be drawn to violent behavior by street families. Which perspective do you agree with? What are some of the characteristics of street families that can make teens safe? Which can make teens more violent?

Chapter 4

1. Kevin Clarke writes that street youth are vulnerable, while Macalane J. Malindi and Linda C. Theron write of the resilience of street teens. Which perspective do you agree with and why?

2. The viewpoint from Toye Olori contends that street youth are a menace to society in Nigeria, but the viewpoint by Evgenia Berezina writes of the victimization of street children by the police. Do you believe that street youth are more often victims or victimizers?

Organizations to Contact

The editors have compiled the following list of organizations concerned with the issues debated in this book. The descriptions are derived from materials provided by the organizations. All have publications or information available for interested readers. The list was compiled on the date of publication of the present volume; the information provided here may change. Be aware that many organizations take several weeks or longer to respond to inquiries, so allow as much time as possible.

Child Welfare League of America (CWLA)
1726 M Street NW, Suite 500, Washington, DC   20036
(202) 688-4200 • fax: (202) 833-1689
website: www.cwla.org

CWLA is an association of nearly eight hundred public and private nonprofit agencies that assist more than 3.5 million abused and neglected children and their families each year with a range of services. The league also works through advocacy and education to shape public policy regarding the welfare of children, and conducts research to determine and disseminate best practices for professionals and volunteers working with children. The league publishes *Children's Voice* magazine, the *Child Welfare Journal*, and hundreds of books. The website offers press releases, research results, and descriptions of programs.

Children of the Night
14530 Sylvan Street, Van Nuys, CA   91411
(818) 908-4474 • fax: (818) 908-1468
website: www.childrenofthenight.org

Children of the Night is a private organization founded in 1979. It is dedicated to assisting children between the ages of 11 and 17 who are forced to prostitute on the streets for food and a place to sleep. The group works with detectives, FBI agents, and prosecutors in cities including Los Angeles, Hollywood, Las Vegas, Seattle, Miami, New York, Minneapolis, Atlanta, Phoenix, and Washington, DC, and provides a 24-hour hotline staffed by trained operators who can help teens find shelter, counseling, and protection.

Covenant House
Times Square Station, New York, NY   10108-0900
hotline: (800) 999-9999
website: www.covenanthouse.org

Covenant House is the largest privately funded nonprofit agency in North and Central America providing shelter and other services to homeless, runaway, and throwaway youth. Its "Nineline" crisis hotline, at 1-800-999-9999, takes free and confidential phone calls from young people, and an online service at www.nineline.org allows young people to post questions and participate in forums and blogs. Incorporated in New York City in 1972, Covenant House International has facilities in 21 cities throughout the United States, Canada, Guatemala, Honduras, Mexico, and Nicaragua. Its website offers information for prospective advocates and volunteers, and a link to its newsletter, *The Covenant House Beacon*.

Family and Youth Services Bureau
US Department of Health and Human Services
Washington, DC   20013
(202) 205-8102 • fax: (202) 260-9333
website: www.acf.hhs.gov/programs/fysb

The mission of the Family and Youth Services Bureau (FYSB) is to provide national leadership on youth and family issues. FYSB's services focus on reducing risks by strengthening families and communities and helping all youth to thrive. Target populations include runaway and homeless youth, victims of family violence, children of prisoners, and youth at risk for early sexual activity. The website features posters, brochures, fact sheets, research reports, and links to other agencies.

National Center for Missing and Exploited Children (NCMEC)
Charles B. Wang International Children's Building
699 Prince Street, Alexandria, VA   22314-3175
(703) 224-2150 • fax: (703) 224-2122
website: www.ncmec.org

Created in 1984, NCMEC is a private nonprofit agency working in cooperation with the US Justice Department to help prevent child abduction and sexual exploitation; help find missing children; and assist child victims of abduction and sexual exploitation, their families, and the professionals who serve them. The agency maintains a 24-hour crisis hotline and a CyberTipline for reporting suspected child victimization. The website features news reports, statistics, testimony, videos, and advice for parents, attorneys, and others.

National Clearinghouse on Families and Youth (NCFY)
P.O. Box 13505, Silver Spring, MD   20911-3505
(301) 608-8098 • fax: (301) 608-8721
e-mail: info@ncfy.com
website: www.ncfy.com

The National Clearinghouse on Families and Youth (NCFY) is a free information service for communities, organizations, and individuals interested in developing new and effective strategies for supporting young people and their families. The Family and Youth Services Bureau (FYSB), US Department of Health and Human Services, established NCFY to link those interested in youth issues with the resources they need to better serve young people, families, and communities. The organization has a library of free and low-cost publications on youth issues; a searchable database with abstracts of thousands of other documents; youth development resources; and a free monthly electronic newsletter.

National Runaway Switchboard
3080 N. Lincoln Ave., Chicago, IL   60657
(773) 880-9860 • fax: (773) 929-5150

e-mail: info@nrscrisisline.org
website: www.1800runaway.org

The National Runaway Switchboard maintains a 24-hour crisis hotline at 1-800-RUNAWAY, which teens may call if they are planning to run away, if they are worried about a friend who has run away, or if they would like help making arrangements to return home. Funded in part through the US Department of Health and Human Services, the organization provides nonjudgmental support to keep young people safe. The website offers articles and advice for teens and parents, a newsletter, and other educational materials.

National Safe Place

2411 Bowman Ave., Louisville, KY   40217
(502) 635-3660 • fax: (502) 635-3678
website: www.nationalsafeplace.org

Safe Place is a national youth outreach program that educates thousands of young people every year about the dangers of running away or trying to resolve difficult, threatening situations on their own. It provides access to immediate help and supportive resources for all young people in crisis through a network of sites sustained by qualified agencies, trained volunteers, and businesses. Cooperating agencies display the yellow Safe Place logo, so that young people in trouble can identify places where they may walk in and obtain help. The website also provides fact sheets, newsletters, reports, and statistics.

National Student Campaign Against Hunger and Homelessness

National Organizing Office, 328 S. Jefferson Street
Suite 620, Chicago, IL   60605
(312) 544-4436 • fax: (312) 275-7150
e-mail: info@studentsagainsthunger.org
website: www.studentsagainsthunger.org

Founded in 1985 by state Public Interest Research Groups (PIRGs), the campaign is committed to ending hunger and homelessness in the United States by educating, engaging, and training high school and college students to meet individuals' immediate needs while advocating for long-term systemic solutions. The organization offers training materials, information about hunger and homelessness, and opportunities for volunteers.

StandUp for Kids
83 Walton Street, Suite 100, Atlanta, GA   30303
(800) 365-4KID • fax: (404) 954-6610
e-mail: contact@standupforkids.org
website: www.standupforkids.org

The mission of StandUp for Kids, an independent organization founded in 1990, is to help homeless and street people age twenty-one and younger. Volunteers in twenty-three states and Washington, DC, identify, befriend, and support young people living on the streets, and work with them in schools and through the Internet to help young people find ways to stay off the street. The website provides short videos, statistical information, and a link to subscribe to the *StandUp for Kids* monthly newsletter.

Bibliography of Books

Sue Books   *Invisible Children in the Society and Its Schools.* Mahway, NJ: Erlbaum, 2007.

Andy Butcher   *Street Children: The Tragedy and Challenge of the World's Millions of Modern-Day Oliver Twists.* Carlisle, UK: Authentic Media, 2003.

CRS Report   *Runaway and Homeless Youth: Demographics, Programs, and Emerging Issues.* Washington, DC: Congressional Research Service, 2007.
for Congress

CRS Report   *The Runaway and Homeless Youth Program: Administration, Funding and Legislative Actions.* Washington, DC: Congressional Research Service, 2006.
for Congress

Kelly Dedel   *Juvenile Runaways.* Washington, DC: Office of Community Oriented Policing Services, 2006.

Patti Feuereisen   *Invisible Girls: The Truth About Sexual Abuse,* 2nd ed. Seattle: Seal Press, 2009.
and Caroline
Pincus

Marni Finkelstein   *With No Direction Home: Homeless Youth on the Road and in the Streets.* Belmont, CA: Wadsworth, 2004.

Claire Fontaine   *Comeback: A Mother and Daughter's Journey Through Hell and Back.* New York: ReganBooks, 2006.
and Mia Fontaine

Jeff Karabanow   *Being Young and Homeless: Understanding How Youth Enter and Exit Street Life*. New York: Peter Lang, 2004.

Natasha Slesnick   *Our Runaway and Homeless Youth: A Guide to Understanding*. Westport, CT: Praeger, 2004.

Emilie Smeaton   *Living on the Edge: The Experiences of Detached Young Runaways*. Leeds, UK: The Children's Society, 2005.

Karen M. Staller   *Runaways: How the Sixties Counterculture Shaped Today's Practices and Policies*. New York: Columbia University Press, 2006.

Judy Westwater and Wanda Carter   *Street Kid*. New York: Harper Element, 2006.

Index

A

Abuse. *See* Drug abuse; Physical abuse; Sexual abuse; Substance abuse

Adaptive preference of street children, 43–45

Adenaike, Wale, 188

ADHD (attention deficit hyperactivity disorder), 19, 29

Affiliation formations by runaways, 26–29

Africa, street children, 171

African American street teens, 100

Ajakaiye, Ade, 190

Alaskan Native street teens, 100

Alcoholism
Midwest runaways, 52
parental alcoholism, 19
teenage runaways, 22–23, 29, 31

Allen, Ernie, 72

Almost Home (Hurley), 144

Amenaghawon, Joseph, 190

American Indian street teens, 100

American Medical Association (AMA), 16–17

Amnesty International, 168

Anchors, Clinton, 72

Antrobus, Rachel, 141, 143

Area Boys street gangs, 186–190
See also Nigeria, menace of street children

Articles 24 and 27 (Convention on the Rights of the Child), 38

Asia, street children, 171

Asian street teens, 100–101, 103

Autonomy, 39–43

B

Babangida, Ibrahim, 189

Baker, D. Nico, 92–96

Ballew, Cori, 122

Barrett, David, 79

Batterham, Philip J., 97–104

Benn, Stanley, 39–40

Berezina, Evgenia, 178–185

Berg, Rose, 143

Bill Wilson Center (CA), 107

Bipolar disorder, 29, 110
See also Mental illness issues

Black Angels (online article), 107

Blaha, Maureen, 52, 54–55, 70, 88–91, 107, 119

Blaw, Ruth, 148

Blazak, Randy, 163

Booth, R., 23

Bowen, Aaron, 125–127

Boyle, Susan, 92–96

Boys
Area Boys street gangs, 186–190
consequences of shelters, 127
fear of arrest, 66
gay youth and sex, 60
home-based sexual abuse, 94, 126
prostitute behavior, 80
Sick Boys street gangs, 158–159

Brazil
execution of children, 172
police brutality, 180–182

Broken families, 144–145

Brown, Sara A., 15

BSI (Brief Symptom Inventory), 100–101

Budnick, Nick, 162

Building Changes (nonprofit organization), 140–141

Burke, Pamela J., 150–156

Burstow, Paul, 111

Bush, George W., 60–61

C

Capecchi, Mario R., 167–168

Casey Family Programs (WA), 143

Caucasian street teens, 100–101, 103

Center for Law and Social Policy (CLASP), 126

Center for Young Adults (WA), 144

Chicago street life, 70

Child pornographers, 78, 83–85

Child Protective Services, 34, 54, 121, 145

Children

    abandonment of, 14–15

    Covenant House statistics, 19–20

    during the Great Depression, 15–16

    execution of, 172

    failure to be reported missing, 70–71

    lack of skills of runaways, 35

    meeting basic needs by running away, 37–39

    self-destructive behavior, 44–45

    See also Convention of the Rights of the Child; Running away, reasons for

Children and Youth Services, Department of (Chicago, IL), 126

Children's Society of the United Kingdom, 109, 111–112, 114

Clarke, Kevin, 169–172

Cocaine, 29, 110

Cochrane, Kira, 109–115

Collegegrad.com, 143

Condom use, 97–98, 100–103

Conduct disorder, 23

Conference of Mayors (US), 127

Congress (US)

    Runaway Youth Act, 16

Convention of the Rights of the Child (CRC), 36, 38–39

Covenant House (New York City), 19, 61, 113

Cowdery, Ken, 126, 134

Crime in the United States, 2008 (US Department of Justice), 82

Cunningham, Kristine, 139–140, 145

D

Daley, Richard M., 124

Dean, Ruth, 79

Denfeld, Rene, 157–164

Depression

    BSI criteria for, 100

    drug use association, 28–29

    gay teens, 53

    HIV risks, 98

    identified in street teens, 23

    LGBT teens, 58

    NCTSN data, 108

    result of street living, 38

Developmental incapacitation of runaways, 37

Dickens, Charles, 14

Drug abuse
crack epidemic, 143
LGBT youth runaways, 58
marijuana use, 29, 52, 68
Midwest runaways, 52
reasons for, 28–29
selling drugs, 67
See also specific drugs by name or group

E

Economic reasons for running away, 65–72

Erikson, Erik, 45

Execution of children, 172

Extortion of street children, 183–184

F

Facebook (website), 19

Faith-based organizations (FBOs), 61

Families
change in home dynamics, 24, 32–34
dynamics of substance abuse, 99–100
economic pressures on, 65
failure to report children missing, 70–71
home-based sexual abuse, 94, 126
parental alcoholism, 19
physical/sexual abuse, 23
throwaway youth, 77–80, 84–86
throwing children out by, 67

Family and Youth Services Bureau (FYSB), 17

FBI National Incident-Based Reporting System (NIBRS), 86–87

FBOs (Faith-based organizations), 61

Fedec, K., 83

Federal Emergency Relief Administration, 16

Federal level recommendations, for LGBT youths, 63

Feinberg, Ted, 52

Females
consciousness-raising programs, 45–46
homeless, with children, 139, 143
Indian women, adaptive preferences, 45
market women, in Nigeria, 188, 190
multiple sexual partners, 101–103
physical/sexual abuse of, 88–91
shelter rules for, 127
street assault data, 90
substance abuse, 102
survival sex data, 94
teenage pregnancy, 91
transitional housing, 133
victimization by pimps, 90

Ferrell, Mary, 69

Finkelhor, David, 86

Fire-setting behavior, 29

Flowers, R. Barri, 77–87

For Runaways, Sex Buys Survival (Urbina), 90

Foster homes
benefits to street teens, 123–136

broken families, 144–145
garbage bag kids, 145–146
older teens cycling back to the streets, 137–149
transition to the streets, 142–144
University of WA study, 146
Fostering Connection to Success Act (2008), 142
Freedom, 39–42, 51

G

Gaetz, Stephen, 81
Gandara, Marla, 97–104
Gangs, 27–28, 44–45
Garbage bag kids, 145–146
Gay and Homeless: In Plain Sight, a Largely Hidden Population, (Zavis), 59
Geraghty, Pauline, 193
Governments
helping children leave the street, 45, 47–49
intervention for Indian women, 45
limitations in providing care, 42–43
providing residential care, 38, 47
Gray, Vanessa, 113–114
Great Depression, 14–16
Green River Killer, 83
Greenwich Village (NY), 16
Grotberg, Edith Henderson, 176
Group homes. *See*, Foster homes.
Guatemala
execution of children, 172, 185

grossly intoxicated children, 180
incest with children, 179

H

Haight-Ashbury (San Francisco), 16
Hallucinogenic drugs, 52
Harlan, Sparky, 107
Harvard University, 128
Haven House Services (NC), 132
Haven W. Poe Runaway Shelter (FL), 120
Health and Human Services, Department of, 17, 58
Heartland Alliance for Human Needs and Human Rights, 125
Hetherington, Amanda, 54
Hierarchy of human needs (Maslow), 36–37, 40–42
Hillier, Carl, 112
HIV-positive individuals, 62, 78
consequences of risky sex, 98
LGBT youth rates, 95
likelihood of running away, 89
runaways vs. at-home peers, 90–91
HMIS (Homeless Management Information System), 135
Holthouse, David, 160
Home for Little Wanderers (MA), 62
Homeless Children and Runaways in the United States Shifflett), 15
Homeless Management Information System (HMIS), 135
Homeless Youth System (OR), 134
Honduras, grossly intoxicated children, 180

Hotline number (1-800-RUNAWAY), 117

Houghton-Brown, Martin, 114

Housing and Urban Development, Department of (US), 63, 141

How System Failed Cynteria, (Whoriskey), 107

Hughes, Alex, 72

Human Rights Watch, 172, 179

Humanist psychology (Maslow), 37

Hunger of runaways, 22, 52

Hurley, Kendra, 144

I

Irvine, Martha, 116–122

J

Jackson, Casi, 138–139

Jacobson, Julie, 144, 146, 148–149

Jaycard, Martin, 70

Jerusalem Post, (newspaper) 35

Jewel (singer), 41

Jewish Chronicle, (newspaper) 35

Joint Center for Housing Studies (Harvard University), 128

Juvenile Justice and Delinquency Prevention, Office of, 90

Juvenile justice system, 59–60

K

King, Tim, 124

Kipling, Rudyard, 14

Klass Kids Foundation, 79

Krai, A., 23

Kutner, Lawrence, 14

L

The Landing (WA), 142–143

Latin America, street children, 171

Latino (US born) street teens, 100–101, 103

Learned helplessness, 43

Lesbian, gay, bisexual, and transgender (LGBT) youth
    dangers of homelessness for, 58–60
    federal level recommendations, 63
    HIV infection rates, 95
    mistreatment in shelters, 61–62
    non-LGB homeless youth vs., 95
    physical/sexual abuse rates, 95
    practitioner level recommendations, 64
    pregnancy rates, 95
    reasons for homelessness, 57
    risks of becoming street teens, 56–64
    risky sexual behaviors, 57, 75
    stark family life conditions, 127
    state/local level recommendations, 63–64
    substance abuse risks, 58, 94–95
    survival sex, 58, 96
    US homeless data, 93–94
    victimization dangers, 59

LGBT (Lesbian, gay, bisexual, and transgender) youth

Lighthouse Youth Services (OH), 131–132

Los Angeles Times (newspaper), 59

Louisiana Office of Child Services, 71

Lukman, Z.M., 79
Lyons, Heather, 134–135

M

Maguire, Melissa, 124
Males
  child abductions in Latin
    America, 181
  fear of, by women runaways,
    66
  multiple sexual partners, 101–
    103
  street assault data, 90
  substance abuse, 102
  survival sex data, 94
  taking advantage of female
    runaways, 31
  transitional housing, 133
Malindi, Macalane J., 173–177
Marijuana use, 23, 25, 29, 52, 68,
  102–103, 160
Martinez, Ruby J., 21–34
Maslow, Abraham, 36–37, 40–42
Maslow Project, 69
McCormick, Megan, 118–119, 121
McCullough, Andy, 194
Mecum, Bob, 131
Medford (OR) street teens, 68
Mehta, Julie, 50–55
Mental illness issues
  bipolar disorder, 29, 110
  conduct disorder, 23
  depression, 19, 23, 29, 38, 53,
    58, 98
  suicidal behavior, 23, 29
Methamphetamines, 52
Mexico
  grossly intoxicated children,
    180

ban on street children
  (Mexico City), 170
Midwest runaways, 52
Milburn, Norweeta G., 97–104
Miles, Bart W., 160
Mockingbird Society (WA), 142
Molnar, B., 23
Moore, Alison, 191–195
Moses, Anne B., 16

N

National Alliance to End Home-
  lessness, 126, 128, 141
National Association of School
  Psychologists, 52
National Center for Missing and
  Exploited Children, 66, 71–72
National Child Traumatic Stress
  Network (NCTSN), 108
National Coalition for the Home-
  less, 57
National Crime Information Cen-
  ter (NCIC), 70–72
National Gay and Lesbian Task
  Force, 57
National Missing Persons Hel-
  pline, 112–113
National Network for Youth, 90
National Runaway Switchboard
  (NRS)
  advice against running away,
    54–55
  calls handled by volunteer
    staffing, 89
  crisis/safety data, 117–118
  funding allocation for, 60, 113
  goals of, 89
  government support for, 119
  LGBT homeless youth data,
    59

limitations of services, 116, 119

means of support for runaways, 75–76

offered services, 19

recommended questions for teens, 51, 54–55

reputation for success, 118

runaway illicit activity data, 67, 75

on traveling by runaways, 70

2000–2007 call growth, 117

National Safe Place (organization), 121

NCIC (National Crime Information Center), 70–72

New Avenues for Youth (OR), 126, 134–135

New York City

attraction for street teens, 16, 70

child prostitution, 85

Covenant House, 19, 61, 113

Port Authority's Youth Services Unit, 70

survival sex data, 94

New York Review of Books (journal), 35

New York Times (newspaper), 90

Newly homeless youth (NHY), 99

NGOs (nongovernmental organizations), 38–39

NHI Shelterforce (website), 144

NIBRS (FBI National Incident-Based Reporting System), 86–87

Nigeria, menace of street children, 186–190

Night Ministry (Chicago), 110, 124, 133–134

Nussbaum, Martha, 37, 45, 48

O

Oliveira, Joanne O'Sullivan, 150–156

Olori, Toye, 186–190

Open Door Youth Shelter, 110

Orion Center, 148

Ormrod, Richard, 86

Overcoming Homelessness Through Healthcare (website), 113

P

Pacific Islander street teens, 100–101, 103

PACT (Public Action for Change Today), 124–125, 135

Panhandling, 14, 67, 75, 160, 162, 170

Parental alcoholism, 19

Peru, resilience of street children, 176

Pew Charitable Trusts, 143

Philippines, execution of children, 172

Physical abuse, 23, 88–91

Physiological needs of children, 40–41

"Pit" street teen community (Cambridge, MA), 150–153

Police brutality against street teens, 180–182

Port Authority's Youth Services Unit (New York City), 70

Portland State University, 163

Post-traumatic stress disorder (PTSD), 146

Practitioner level recommendations, for LGBT youths, 64

Preference deformation of street children, 44

Pregnancy
  foster care teens, 143
  incentives for, 138, 140
  LGBT street teens, 94
  as reason for running away, 53, 75, 127
  risks for street teens, 192
  of street teens, 30–31, 91

Prostitution by street teens, 77–87
  average age at entry, 79–80
  child pornography and, 85
  child sexual abuse and, 81
  exploitation by adults, 46
  female vs. male, 87
  National Network for Youth data, 90–91
  1999–2008 juvenile arrest records, 82
  NRS data, 75
  police contact and, 85–87
  reasons for turning to, 23, 67, 78
  risks of murder, 82–83
  San Francisco teens, 51
  varied risks for youths, 78
  violent encounters, 81–83

Prostitution of Children and Child-Sex Tourism (report), 84

Public Action for Change Today (PACT), 124–125, 135

Putnam, Mark, 140

R

Railway Children, 193
Ramsay, Susie, 192
Randall, Cleveland, 71
Rape, 31
Ray, Nicholas, 56–64
Rebeiro, M.O., 182

Renegade Kids, Suburban Outlaws (Blazak), 163

Resilience in Street Children and in Victims of Political Violence in Peru (Grotberg), 176

Right to Shelter law (NV), 120

Risks of running away
  becoming invisible, 72
  developmental incapacitation, 37
  fleeing from pain, 53–54
  for gay/transgender teens, 56–64
  hunger, 22, 52
  lack/loss of autonomy, 42–43
  not meeting physiological needs, 40–41
  panhandling, 14, 67, 75, 160, 162, 170
  physical/sexual abuse, 88–91
  pregnancy, 53
  promiscuity, 22–23
  rape, violence, 31
  street dangers, 23–24
  substance abuse, 22–23, 28–29, 31–32
  trauma, psychological, 38

Robinson, Steven, 107
Roman, Nan, 128
Roosevelt, Franklin D., 16
ROOTS (WA), 138–139, 145, 148
Rosenthal, Doreen, 97–104
Rotheram-Borus, Mary Jane, 97–104
Rowell, Victoria, 130

Runaway, Homeless, and Missing Children Protection Act (RHMCPA), 60

Runaway and Homeless Youth Act (RHYA) programs, 63, 129, 131

Runaway Helpline (Great Britain), 113–114

Runaway Lives (online forum), 75

Runaway Youth Act, 16

The Runaway Youth Act: Paradoxes of Reform (Moses), 16

Runaways at Risk (Moore), 193

Running away, reasons for
   abuse, physical and sexual, 23, 36
   change in home dynamics, 24, 32–34
   creation of new affiliations, 26–29
   escape from dangerous situations, 25
   family conflicts, 53
   gangs and gang affiliation, 27–28, 44–45
   illness of parent, 27
   on impulse, 25–26
   lack of parental care, 24–25
   meeting basic needs, 37–39
   mental illness issues, 23, 29
   poverty, neglect, 36
   pregnancy, 53
   search for less restrictive environment, 22, 24

Rural Child Dependency, Neglect, and Delinquency (Brown), 15

Russia, grossly intoxicated children, 180

S

Safe and Sound Campaign (United Kingdom), 111–112

Salomonsen-Sautel, Stacy, 92–96

San Francisco street life, 51, 70

Schimmel, Noam, 35–49

Schissel, B., 83

Schnars, Matt, 132–133

Sen, Amartya, 37

Sexual abuse
   home-based, of boys, 94, 126
   home-based, of girls, 126
   incest in Guatemala, 179
   LGBT youth rates, 95
   prostituted children and, 81
   rape, 31
   as reason for running away, 23, 36
   street teen females, 88–91

Sexual behavior
   multiple partners, 101–103
   non-home increased sexual activity, 101–102
   risks for LGBT youth, 58–60
   risks for street teens, 97–104
   substance abuse association, 102–104
   trading sex for basic needs, 91
   See also Prostitution by street teens; Survival sex

Sexually transmitted diseases (STDs), 98, 103

Shade, S., 23

Shelters for runaways, 14, 53
   Basic Center Programs, 61
   Bill Wilson Center, 107
   concerns about restrictive rules, 33–34
   Covenant House, 19–20, 61
   CRC provision, 38–39
   education profile of teens, 91
   educational aspect, 44
   Home for Little Wanderers, 62
   homelessness program problems, 60–61
   Maslow Project, 69
   Maslow's hierarchy component, 40

mistreatment of LGBT youths, 61–62

Roosevelt's establishment of, 16

transitional living programs, 60

understaffing concerns, 47

United Kingdom, limited shelters, 111–112

US network, 110–111

Shifflett, Peggy A., 15

Sick Boys street gangs, 158–159

Smeaton, Emilie, 111

Smith, Carol, 137–149

Smith, Cynthia, 121

Snyder, Betty, 68–69

Social and Economic Rights Action (SERAC), 190

Social cognitive theory, 99–100

Social services, 38

Societal neglect of street children, 185

Solorio, M. Rosa, 97–104

South African street children, 44

Spangenberg, Mia, 85

STDs (sexually transmitted diseases), 98, 103

"Street Children and Their Relationship with the Police" (Rebeiro), 182

Street Connect (website), 14–15

Street families
    creation of violent teens, 157–164
    environmental conditions, 152–154
    freedoms and dangers, 155–156
    Internet spread of family culture, 161–162

"Pit" street teen community, 150–153

relationship dynamics, 151–152

safety for street teens, 150–156

Wicca ritualistic religion, 152–154

Street Life Is No Life for Children (Jewel), 41

Street Life on Mill study (Miles), 160

Street Life—and Death (Budnick), 162

Stromberg, Meghan, 123–136

Substance abuse
    cocaine, 29, 110
    family dynamics and risks, 99–100
    hallucinogenic drugs, 52
    male/female sexual partners, 102
    marijuana, 23, 25, 29, 52, 68, 102–103, 160
    Midwest runaways, 52

Success Stories: Victoria Rowell (fostercaremonth.com), 130

Suicidal behavior and attempts, 23, 29

Survival sex, 22, 79
    child pornographers and, 84
    defined, 91, 93
    LGBT vs. heterosexual teens, 58, 96
    meeting basic needs from, 78
    social capital and, 155
    street teen rates, 94

T

Tattersall, Clare, 85
10 Year Plan to End Homelessness, 124
Thomas, Shane, 141
Thomson, Melissa, 79
Throwaway youth, 77–80, 84–86
Tinubu, Bola, 189
Together Center (WA), 139
Torres, Tony, 141, 145
Transitional Age Youth Initiative (San Francisco), 141
Transitional living programs (TLPs), 60, 123, 130–131
Trauma, psychological, 38

U

UN Convention of the Rights of the Child, 36, 38
UN Millennium Challenge Project, 170, 172
UN Office on Drugs and Crime, 187–188
UN Special Rapporteur, 181
UNICEF (United Nations International Children's Emergency Fund), 168
United Kingdom
    aid by community nurses, 191–195
    Children's Society, 109, 111–112, 114, 192
    emulating US shelter network, 109–115
    life for young runaways, 193
    limited shelters for runaways, 111–112
    Railway Children, 193
    runaway data (2010), 193
    safe houses, 193–194
United States
    Child Protective Services, 34, 54, 121, 145
    Conference of Mayors, 127
    Haven House Services, 132
    Haven W. Poe Runaway Shelter, 120
    Homeless Youth System, 134
    Lighthouse Youth Services, 131
    National Safe Place organization, 121
    network of shelters, 110–111
    New Avenues for Youth, 126, 134–135
    Night Ministry charity, 110, 124, 133–134
    Open Door Youth Shelter, 110
    Public Action for Change Today, 124–125, 135
    Right to Shelter law, 120
    ROOTS young adult shelter, 138–139, 145, 148
    Runaway and Homeless Youth Act, 63, 129, 131
    transitional living programs, 60, 123, 130–131
    Youth Service Bureau, 121
University of Colorado Denver College of Nursing, 21
Urban Peak (CO), 92
Urbina, Ian, 65–72
USA Today Magazine, 41

V

Van Leeuwen, James M., 92–96
Vets Edge, 139
Violence on the streets, 31, 71, 81–83

Vulnerabilities of street teens,
169–172

W

Wagner, Victoria, 119
Walker, Nancy, 79
Wallace, Denise, 143
Washington, Harvey, 90
Washington state of
    Casey Family Programs, 143
    Center for Young Adults, 144
    The Landing, 142–143
    Mockingbird Society, 142
    ROOTS, 138–139, 145, 148
    Together Center, 139

Watters, J., 23
Weiss, Robert E., 97–104
Whoriskey, Peter, 107
Wicca ritualistic religion, 152–154
Williams, Tray, 71

Y

Youth Homelessness Team, 124
Youth in Transition Database, 135
Youth Service Bureau (IN), 121
Youth Shelter Network, 124

Z

Zavis, Alexandra, 59